VANISHING

HERITAGE

NOTES AND QUERIES ABOUT THE ARCHAEOLOGY AND CULTURE HISTORY OF LICKING COUNTY , OHIO

EDITORS

PAUL E. HOOGE   AND   *BRADLEY T. LEPPER*

CONTRIBUTIONS   BY

WILLAM S. DANCEY, PhD
PAUL E. HOOGE
BRADLEY T. LEPPER, PhD
PAUL J. PACHECO
DEE ANN WYMER, PhD

PHOTOGRAPHY   BY
KENT   BOWSER
with contributions from JEFF EDWARDS and PAUL HOOGE

COPY EDITOR - ANN BREMNER
COVER   ART - PAT CHENEY
LAYOUT and DESIGN - ANDREW HOOGE

This book was produced with assistance from:
THE OHIO HUMANITIES COUNCIL and PAUL and JILL GRIESSE
A Publication of
The Licking County Archaeology and Landmarks Society

VANISHING
HERITAGE

Published by LCALS

First Printing
September 1992

Library of Congress Catalog Card Number: 92 - 85574

ISBN: 0-9634331-0-5

**NOTES AND QUERIES ABOUT THE ARCHAEOLOGY AND
CULTURE HISTORY OF LICKING COUNTY, OHIO**

TABLE OF CONTENTS

EDITORS   INTRODUCTION

Archaeological resources are extremely fragile, sometimes lying directly on the surface or protected only by a few inches of soil. Most of what remains of an entire habitation site can be totally obliterated by one pass of a bulldozer's blade.

The archaeological record in Ohio has been mixed and blended by over a century of cultivation on the fertile plains and terraces where prehistoric Native Americans made their homes for over ten thousand years. In many cases, these artifact rich fields have been picked clean of almost all traces of the past by generations of passers-by and tenacious collectors who, after spring rains, harvest the past from freshly cultivated surfaces.

Hundreds of burial mounds and geometric enclosures were documented across Central and Southern Ohio during the early nineteenth century. Today, few remain intact and most have been plowed flat or built over. The largest complex of geometric earthworks in the world once spread gracefully over the landscape where Newark, Ohio is now located. Two major features of the five square mile system remain today; the rest have, for the most part, been eliminated or exist as traces noticeable only faintly in old aerial photographs.

No single element has caused the demise of Ohio's archaeological past, but certainly an ignorance of the value of the resource to this and future generations has been a contributing factor. Vanishing Heritage provides information about one of the state's richest archaeological regions - Licking County. The authors attempt to fill in some important gaps in the literature and to expand in others. All of the authors have been involved in on-going research in Licking County through a cooperative effort with The Licking County Archaeology and Landmarks Society and faculty and students from The Ohio State University Department of Anthropology. The Licking County Archaeology and Landmarks Society was organized in 1983 to facilitate research and develop educational programs about archaeology in the Central Ohio area.

It is hoped that Vanishing Heritage will help to inform the public, as well as students of archaeology, about the need to be more aware of the fragile nature of the archaeological resource and to assist wherever and whenever possible in preserving it.

CHAPTER I
AN OVERVIEW

Willam S. Dancey

Sixteen thousand years ago most of Licking County was covered by ice. In fact, the glaciers of the Pleistocene Epoch—the Ice Age—had blanketed the region for nearly ten thousand years. At approximately this time, however, the ice began to melt, slowly exposing the land surface and opening it to human colonization. As the ice sheet retreated (a process termed "deglaciation"), humans and other animals, moved north to establish footholds on the glacial deposits of sand, silt, and gravel. At first vegetation was sparse and the terrain open. Herd animals such as mammoth and caribou were common. Eventually, denser forests covered the landscape, providing habitats for animals such as deer. By 2000 B.C. the environment had come to resemble that of nineteenth-century Ohio, with similar climatic conditions and many of the same plants and animals established in the region.

Through their research, archaeologists have been able to trace changes in the patterns of life among the human inhabitants of the deglaciated landscape. Based on major shifts in such "lifeways," archaeologists distinguish five major periods: the Paleoindian period (12,000–6000 B.C.), the Archaic period (6000–1000 B.C.), the Woodland period (1000 B.C.–A.D. 1000), the Late Prehistoric period (1000–1650), and the Historic period (1650-1850). Some of these periods are also subdivided further: for example, archaeologists often distinguish "Early," "Middle," and "Late" phases of the Woodland period. Initially, during the Paleoindian/Archaic periods (figure 1), the human inhabitants lived in small groups. Their diet was based upon foods that could be acquired by hunting and collecting, and the groups moved frequently throughout the year. Weather, animal migrations, and seasonal variations in plant food availability all contributed to their nomadic habits. As the modern environment became established, changes in the archaeological record indicate that the descendants of these early societies became more stationary and developed cultural practices associated with sedentary life. Thus emerged the Woodland period, characterized by the domestication of many local plants and noted for its burial mounds and geometric earthworks. During the Late Prehistoric period, patterns of food production appear to have changed significantly. Maize (corn) and other non-local food crops known as "tropical cultigens" emerged in many places and came to dominate the cultural geography. The beginning of the Historic period marks the approximate time when Euro-African populations (that is, those from the continents of Europe and Africa) began to spill over the Appalachian mountains and come into contact with the descendants of the earlier Native societies. Many of these groups had already felt the impact contact with the new settlers brought to their lifeways and living conditions. Native groups had no acquired immunity to European diseases such as small pox, for example, and suffered devastating losses when exposed to them. By 1850 most surviving Native people had been forcibly removed from the Ohio region, and the land had been incorporated into the developing United States.

Burial mounds and geometric earthworks provide the most visible evidence of prehistoric human occupation in the Licking County area. These ancient "monuments," as they were referred to by early archaeologists, are tangible clues to prehistoric population numbers and densities, at least for the societies of the periods when they were constructed. But these ceremonial and funerary sites are not the only available sources of information. Traces of prehistoric domestic settlements, such as camps and villages, also are visible, as are what might be called "industrial" sites such as the quarries where flint was acquired. The study of such sites can provide insight into many facets of past lifeways and social organization. The evidence they offer can help us learn about the sizes of local groups, the permanent or temporary nature of their settlements, the techniques they used to procure food and other resources, and the ways they might have manufactured the goods they needed. Information from domestic, industrial, ceremonial, and funerary sites, taken together and combined with estimates of the sites' ages, will enable us to develop a more comprehensive picture of past social life and cultural history.

Despite its potential richness, the archaeology of Licking County has not yet been explored thoroughly or systematically. Nevertheless, the archaeological record of this region may well hold answers to many intriguing questions.

How soon after deglaciation did colonization occur? Was it by established populations from the south or by new groups migrating out of Asia? What foods were first eaten, and how did they influence the way of life of the early inhabitants? By what processes were new plant foods added to the diet? How, and why, were local plants domesticated in the Woodland period, and why did this precede the appearance of tropical cultigens? What role did ceramic containers, which appear only about 3,000 years ago, play in changing methods of food storage and cooking? The later phases of the Woodland period witnessed the development of year-round villages and an increased importance given to maize and squash in agriculture. How did these events set the stage for the emergence of the maize-beans-squash system of field agriculture, and what impact did this system have on the forest and the landscape as a whole?

These are some of the many questions that can be posed about the 14,000 years of human occupation in Licking County and neighboring regions. Recent fieldwork coupled with the results of previous work show that it is possible to gain systematic knowledge of cultural history and past lifeways in this area. After decades of neglect, the time has come for archaeological methods to be applied extensively and intensively to this part of Ohio.

This book brings together a series of articles about the archaeology of Licking County. Some summarize discoveries from organized expeditions of recent years. Others report for the first time the results of excavations done years ago. Specific sites (the Murphy Site, the Newark Earthworks, and the Alligator Mound) are discussed in some and special topics (such as Middle Woodland plant foods) in others. Because an exploding population and intensifying land use threaten to destroy or severely damage many archaeologically sensitive sites in Licking County, the issue of preservation is given special attention. We hope that these essays will provide a representative sample of current information on the region's prehistory and early history and will illuminate the nature of the archaeological remains upon which this knowledge is based. We also hope to suggest directions for future research and reasons why active programs of preservation, conservation, and protection should be undertaken in the county.

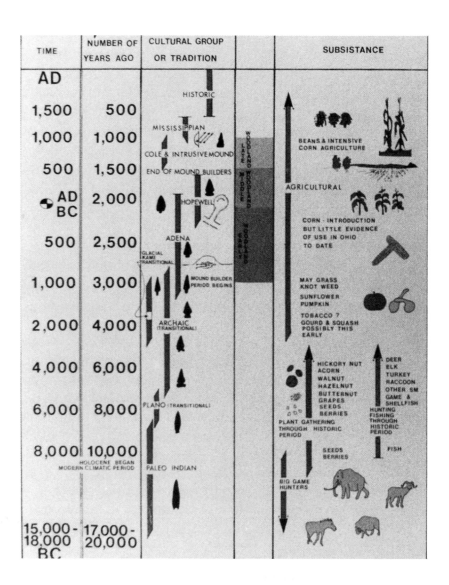

Figure 1.
Chronology of Ohio's Prehistoric Native Americans

CHAPTER II
PALEOINDIAN PIONEERS:

Bradley T. Lepper

Humans are relative newcomers to the Americas. In spite of the claims that occasionally appear in pseudoscientific literature, it is generally acknowledged that humans did not evolve in the New World. Fossil skeletons from the Old World document the gradual evolution of the human species. By contrast, all the fossil skeletons ever documented from the Americas represent fully modern humans. Raymond Dart, Robert Broom, Louis and Mary Leaky, and many other dedicated scholars have demonstrated that the human story began in Africa more than three million years ago. In succeeding millennia human ancestors migrated out of Africa and into the more rigorous climates of Asia and Europe, where increasingly sophisticated technologies were required for existence. Shelter, clothing, and control of fire, for example, were necessary before humans could survive through the harsh winters of the northern latitudes. But once people had pushed northward onto the Siberian plains—between 70,000 and 40,000 years ago—they unknow ingly were on the threshold of a "New World."

Thousands of miles of ocean had separated the Americas from the tropical Old World since long before the dawn of humanity. Only in the far north, where the narrow Bering Strait divides Siberia from Alaska, is it possible to see the New World from the Old. During the Pleistocene Epoch—the Ice Age—lowered sea levels opened up the expansive land bridge connecting these two great land masses. Scientists call this exposed portion of the continental shelf Beringia. The emergence of Beringia would have allowed Paleoindians to walk from Asia into the New World. Scholars since Thomas Jefferson have concluded that Alaska was the original gateway to the Americas.

The earliest human occupation of the Americas is poorly under-stood, and scholars agree on few generalizations. But it is accepted that modern Native Americans are descended from Asian immigrants. It is also widely accepted that humans were present in the New World by at least 11,500 years ago. Archaeological evidence for occupation at that time takes the form of a distinctive type of tool—the Clovis fluted spear point (figure 2)—that is unique to the Americas. Characterized by a long groove, or flute, chipped from the base of the point, Clovis points and associated stone and bone tools have been found from Alaska to northern South America. In many widely scattered areas where these tools have been found, they have been reliably dated using radiocarbon methods to a relatively brief period, lasting from about 11,500 to 10,500 years ago.

However, these generally accepted facts leave many fundamental questions regarding the origins of Clovis technology unresolved. No fluted points have been documented from Asia. Consequently, fluted points must have been invented by early Americans sometime after their arrival on this continent. The fact that fluted points occur virtually simultaneously across the Americas may be explained in either of two ways. Either *people*, carrying these distinctive tools, invented shortly after their arrival in Alaska, spread very rapidly across an unpopulated continent, or the *idea* of making fluted points spread very rapidly through peoples who already were occupying the Americas. If the latter is true, then traces of earlier "pre-Clovis" occupations should be present.

The important South American sites of Monte Verde and Pedra Furada indicate that people were present in the New World at least 14,000 years ago and perhaps as early as 30,000 years ago. But where is the

Figure 2.   *Bowser*
The Clovis point from Granville Township in Licking Co. represents the earliest period of prehistorics human occupation and tool manufacturing in Ohio.

evidence for such early human habitation in North America? If Paleoindians entered the New World through Beringia, then they must have traveled through North America in order to reach South America. Meadowcroft Rockshelter in western Pennsylvania has yielded the most persuasive evidence for a pre-Clovis occupation in the Ohio valley. The deeply stratified deposits at Meadowcroft have produced a continuous record of human occupation extending back perhaps 20,000 years. Systematic archaeological investigations in Licking County and neighboring areas may uncover evidence of similar early occupations here.

Regardless of precisely when humans first discovered the Americas, the world into which they wandered belonged to the Ice Age. Vast sheets of glacial ice blanketed much of North America including most of present-day Licking County. These enormous continental ice sheets had obvious (and not so obvious) consequences for the climate of Ohio throughout the Pleistoscene Epoch. Obviously, Ice Age summers were colder than those of today due, in part, to the proximity of the giant glaciers to the north. As a result, plants and animals typical of tundra and northern, or boreal, forest environments were able to live in Ohio.

Suprisingly, Ohio winters in the Ice Age were not as cold and harsh as they are today. The dwindling mountains of glacial ice that covered most of Canada prevented the cold arctic air masses from sweeping southward across the Ohio valley. (Try to imagine a winter without "Alberta Clippers" hurling bitter winter storms down from the Arctic!) Since winters were relatively mild, plants and animals of the southern forests could share the landscape with species more characteristic of the tundra and boreal forest.

Ice Age Ohio would seem a strange and unfamiliar place to a twentieth-century resident. It would have resembled neither the forests of modern Ohio nor the evergreen forests of southern Ontario. Somehow the landscape would have combined plants and animals from various environments into a crazy-quilt pattern of mixed deciduous and coniferous woodlands and open meadows. But the strangest and most unfamiliar aspect of this world would have been the many species of giant mammals: mammoths, mastodons, giant ground sloths, giant beaver, and fearsome predators such as the saber-toothed cat, the American lion, and the short-faced bear. These and dozens of other remarkable animal species roamed across the Ohio countryside when the distant ancestors of Licking County's Moundbuilders first took up residence in our rolling hills and valleys.

Why have these majestic animals vanished from the American landscape? Some scholars argue that the first Americans were ferocious big game hunters who swept across the hemisphere on a killing spree, exterminating the giant mammals. Evidence from sites in the American Southwest and from as far east as Missouri indicates that early inhabitants preyed upon some Ice Age mammals. But it is not reasonable to suppose that Stone Age hunters and gatherers could have slaughtered dozens of species of big game. The capacity and appalling proclivity for driving animals into extinction on such a vast scale seems peculiar to modern humans. It is certainly revealing to note that the most intensively hunted animal in prehistoric North America—the bison—did not become extinct! A more likely explanation for the disappearance of the wide range of Ice Age animals is that they fell victim to the drastic climatic changes that ended this era.

The earliest Ohioans about whom much is known were the fluted point wielding hunters and gatherers who first appeared in this region late in the Ice Age. Archaeologists refer to these people as Paleoindians. Paleoindians in Ohio had a rich variety of food sources from which to choose, and we should not assume that they would have arbitrarily restricted their diet to mastodon steaks such as those which were carved off the Burning Tree Mastodon (figure 3) discovered in a peat bog south of Newark. Indeed, there is now evidence from Eastern sites that Paleoindians ate nuts and berries, fish, deer, caribou, and a variety of small game animals—in addition to an occasional mastodon.

The chronology of the early Paleoindian occupation of the Ohio valley is uncertain. Currently, there are no reliable radiocarbon-dated fluted-point sites in all of midcontinental North America. Based on dated sites in southwestern and eastern North America we can surmise that early Paleoindian peoples lived in Ohio between 11,500 and 10,500 years ago.

The detailed study of the distribution of fluted points within Licking County has only begun, and important traces of Paleoindian pioneers surely remain hidden beneath the surface of our fertile fields. Recent archaeological investigations at the Munson Springs Site near Granville (figure4) have uncovered evidence for what may have been one of the earliest settlements in Licking County. An unfinished fluted point was found here deeply buried beneath soil containing the artifacts of many latter peoples. Since the evidence of Paleoindian occupation is buried and has not been disturbed by the plow or recent construction activities, this site may yield important clues about the way of life of the ancient Ice Age peoples. Because so much of what we think we know about these groups is based on such a meager amount of data, continued research at the site may radically change our understanding of Paleoindians and their world.

Edwards

Figure 3   In December of 1989, an almost complete skeleton of an American Mastodon was discovered in south-central Licking County. Evidence indicates that the Burning Tree Mastodon was butchered.

Hooge

Figure 4

The Munson Spring Site in Granville, Ohio was occupied at one point by Paleo Indians about 11,000 years ago. This area attracted prehistoric Native Americans throughout the prehistoric period.

CHAPTER III

THE LEGACY OF THE LICKING RIVER BASIN MOUNDBUILDERS:

Paul Pacheco

INTRODUCTION

The Native Americans popularly known as the Moundbuilders are easily the best-known prehistoric inhabitants of the land that makes up present-day Licking County, just as the burial mounds and other earthworks they constructed are the most-noted archaeological features of the area. However, surprisingly little archaeological research has been conducted to provide a legitimate understanding of the societies responsible for these well-known ancient monuments.

One reason that we know so little about the Moundbuilders is that many mounds and earthworks were destroyed prior to the introduction of modern standards of scientific archaeological excavation and reporting. Numerous Licking County mounds have been "dug-into" during the last 150 years, but a majority of these excavations were carried out by zealous collectors and amateur archaeologists mainly interested in the ancient treasures they believed to be buried in the mounds. Professional archaeologists of the nineteenth and early twentieth centuries, though they usually made some effort to publicize the results of their excavations, were motivated by essentially the same interests. They too concentrated on amassing and cataloguing collections of artifacts rather than on studying and documenting the total context in which such artifacts were found. In addition, even careful archaeological research has tended to emphasize the study of mounds and earthworks to the virtual exclusion of other sites, such as habitation or daily living sites, associated with the Moundbuilders. Only during the last two decades have some archaeologists begun extensive research and excavations at Moundbuilder habitation sites such as Licking County's Murphy Site (which is the subject of

Chapter four).

The Moundbuilders of Licking County did not exist in isolation. Mound-building peoples lived in many areas of the East and Midwest, and shared lifeways transcending the contemporary boundaries of counties and states. Archaeologists distinguish several concentrations of Moundbuilders in the Ohio Valley, sometimes identifying such groups by reference to geographic features of the locations in which they lived. One population that can be defined in this way lived in the vicinity of the Licking River and its tributaries; an area described as the Licking River basin. The Moundbuilders of the Licking River basin and those of other areas such as the Miami and Scioto river basins maintained some degree of genetic and cultural independence from one another even while participating in a shared ideological system that included the building of mounds and earthworks.

From the confluence of its North and South Fork tributaries near Newark, the Licking River flows east to join the Muskingum River, which then flows south to the Ohio. About seventy-five percent of the Licking River basin, which encompasses a total of 779 square miles, is located in present-day Licking County, with portions also located in Muskingum, Knox, Fairfield, and Perry Counties. The Licking River basin has considerable variation in topography, due in part to its location at the edge of the farthest advance of the Late Pleistocene glaciers. The western portion of the drainage basin, which was covered by the glaciers, ranges from relatively level to gently sloping terrain. The central portion contains the remains of glaciated bedrock hills which provide relatively steep margins for stream valleys filled with glacial sediments. The Newark Earthworks, (figure 5) the largest geometrical mound and earthwork concentration in the world, is located on such terraces formed by glacial deposits. The unglaciated eastern portion of the basin—the area never reached by the glaciers—has rugged topography with steep hills, long narrow ridges, and narrow stream valleys. Flint Ridge, an important source of raw materials for prehistoric stone tools, is located in the rugged unglaciated terrain fifteen miles southeast of the Newark Earthworks.

The combination of such natural resources with a hospitable climate may account for the significant concentration of Moundbuilder sites in the Licking River basin. At the time of the Moundbuilders, the

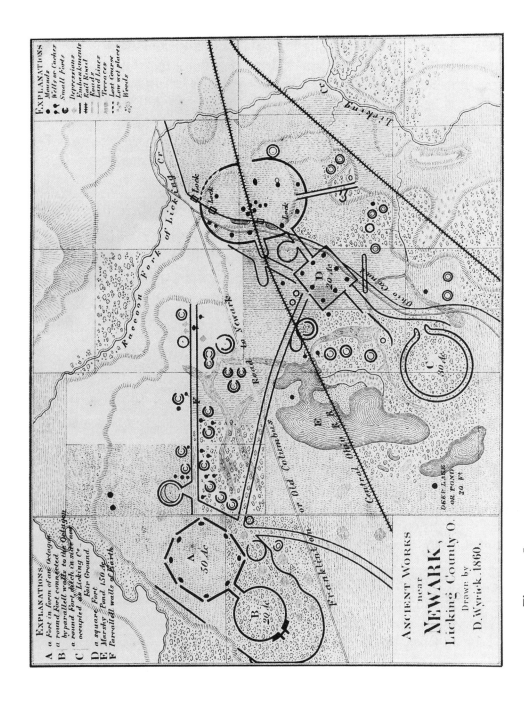

Figure 5   One of the most accurate maps of the Newark Earthworks was drawn by
surveyor, David Wyrick sometime late in the 1850's.

temperate climate and abundant rainfall of the Licking region provided living conditions for rich, diverse flora (plants) and fauna (animals). Reconstructions of the flora of the region for the last two thousand years indicate the existence of a birch-maple forest. Oaks and hickories were also abundant on well - drained soils and slopes. The climate was generally similar to that of today, although some evidence suggests a trend towards cooler and drier conditions toward the end of the Mound - building period.

Most, if not all, of the mound-building activity in the Licking River basin occurred over a relatively concentrated period between about 400 B.C. and A.D. 400, although mounds continued to be built for several centuries in other regions of the eastern United States.

In terms of the time periods contemporary archaeologists use to indicate major changes in the archaeological record, mound-building activities in the Licking basin, and in central Ohio generally, began during the later stages of the Early Woodland period (1000 B.C. to 100 B.C.) and continued throughout the Middle Woodland period (100 B.C. to 400 A.D.).

Some evidence suggests that a flurry of mound building occurred in the Licking region at about 200 B.C. The mounds built at this time were primarily conical in shape and located individually, dispersed throughout valley and upland locations. This Early Woodland pattern of dispersed single mounds evolved during the Middle Woodland period into a pattern in which larger regional and subregional complexes of mounds and geometric earthworks were centralized in and near main stream valleys.

ADENA AND HOPEWELL

Archaeologists have long categorized the mounds of central Ohio as associated with either of two cultural groups who appear to have been active in the central Ohio valley during the Early and Middle Woodland period and whose mound-building activities roughly conform to the patterns described above. These mound-building cultures are referred to as Adena and Hopewell, terms taken from the locations of and the names given to mounds once thought to be representative of each culture. All mounds excavated to date in the Licking River basin have been attributed to one or the other of these two groups. Single conical mounds are the most common Adena constructions, with groups of mounds and small earthworks being less common. Larger-scale and more-elaborate earthwork complexes, most dated to after 100 B.C., are identified as Hopewell. The greatest number of Adena burial mounds are located in central Ohio; mounds and earthworks considered Hopewell have been found over larger areas of Ohio and in other states including Illinois, where archaeologists have identified a Hopewell-type culture referred to as the Havana Tradition. In the Licking River basin and elsewhere, Adena mounds and earthworks are found in many kinds of locations: in main river valleys, along small tributaries, and elsewhere in the hinterland. Hopewell sites are generally found in the vicinity of main river valleys. The artifacts or cultural objects found in association with Moundbuilder sites also have often been categorized as Adena or Hopewell, with the latter term usually applied to the more complex and elaborate objects.

A great deal of confusion surrounds the Adena and Hopewell designations despite their long-standing and wide-spread use. The most difficult issue involves the relationship between the two groups. To many archaeologists, Adena constructions and artifacts appear to represent the beginning of a cultural tradition that continues and evolves into Hopewell. In this interpretation, the terms describe different eras or phases of one continuing group—in simple terms, one might say that the "Adena" were the ancestors of the "Hopewell." The problem is that several "late" radiocarbon dates (after 100 B.C.) associated with sites identified as Adena appear to contradict this simple description, indicating instead that at least some Adena and Hopewell constructions and objects must have been produced at about the same time.

This has led some archaeologists to suggest that Adena and Hopewell mounds, earthworks, and artifacts must represent the work of competing and distinct contemporaneous groups or societies. They theorize that Adena populations were displaced from central Ohio by Hopewell populations who may even have immigrated into the area from other regions such as Illinois. Perhaps some local Adena groups continued to exist along with Hopewell groups, refusing to join the new trade and ceremonial networks; others might have adopted Hopewell lifeways introduced by newcomers from the Havana Tradition. Other scholars argue that Adena populations changed and "became" Hopewell as a result of a diffusion of ideas from the Havana Tradition, again with some local Adena groups refusing to participate in the new system and being displaced to the south and east.

No firm archaeological evidence supports the theory of immigration and resulting displacement in the Licking River basin. Instead the regional theme is clearly one of cultural continuity, regardless of whether one uses the terms "Adena" and "Hopewell" to describe earlier and later phases of a continuing sequence or to identify different but concurrent manifestations of the mound-building tradition. Consequently other theories must be explored and tested in order to more accurately explain the relationship between Adena and Hopewell. In one such interpretation, the Adena designation is seen as describing a loosely defined burial program common to small local groups in the central and upper Ohio River Valley. At the same time that populations continued the mound-building practices associated with this program, they may have begun to participate in the construction of the centralized regional earthwork complexes identified as Hopewell. Contemporaneous Adena and Hopewell constructions from the transitional period of about 100 B.C. to A.D. 100 might have been functionally distinct productions of one continuing and evolving culture. What have been called Adena mounds could have functioned at the local or community level while Hopewell earthworks began to function at the regional level. Such a view is consistent with current perceptions of Hopewell as a loosely organized ideological system in which regional societies throughout the eastern United States participated to different extents.

The difficulties presented by the use of the Adena and Hopewell designations stem from the inflexible standards employed in defining each type. The Rutledge Mound, which was located six miles southeast of Newark on an isolated hilltop, illustrates this problem. This mound's conical shape and its location on an upland hilltop, rather than in a main stream valley, fit the pattern usually designated as Adena. Yet excavations at this mound revealed artifacts that could be assigned to both Adena and Hopewell traditions. One copper animal figure or effigy (figure 6) in particular has seemed to some scholars a classic Hopewell artifact, leading them to consider the mound to be a Hopewell construction. A radiocarbon date of 260 B.C. (based on a charred log associated with this artifact) was rejected, because such a date is considered too "early" for a Hopewell mound. The desire to label the mound either Adena or Hopewell has clouded the potential that this site presents for understanding the changing and evolving cultural traditions in the region.

MOUNDS

The practice of building both mounds and earthworks was apparently well established in the Licking River basin, although, as one might expect, individual mounds far out number larger geometric earthwork complexes. Perhaps as many as 300 mounds were located in the Licking River basin during prehistoric times. As recently as 1914 William C. Mills, curator and director of the Ohio State Archaeological and Historical Society (the precursor to the Ohio Historical Society), listed the locations of 225 Licking County mounds in his *Archaeological Atlas of Ohio* (figure 8). Recent literature and physical mounds surveys have confirmed locations for mounds in the county, and, in Ohio, Licking County is second only to Ross County in its concentration of mounds.

Of these mounds, eight are known to have been built of stone and 56 of earth. The construction materials of the other known mounds have not been ascertained. Mounds had considerable variety in size and shape, but the majority had the conical shape that has been regarded as typical of Adena construction. Evidence from excavated conical-shaped mounds in the region suggests that such mounds were built in stages over a relatively long period of time, a pattern archaeologists also have noted in examples of Adena mounds from other sections of the Ohio valley. Existing measurements for 97 mounds suggest an average size of about ten feet high and fifty feet in diameter.

The diverse topography in the Licking River basin provided a multitude of options for the placement of mounds and earthworks. In general, mounds were located either at the summit of higher ground or on a stream terrace. Upland mounds dominate the pattern in the unglaciated portion of the drainage, probably due to the lack of wide floodplains or

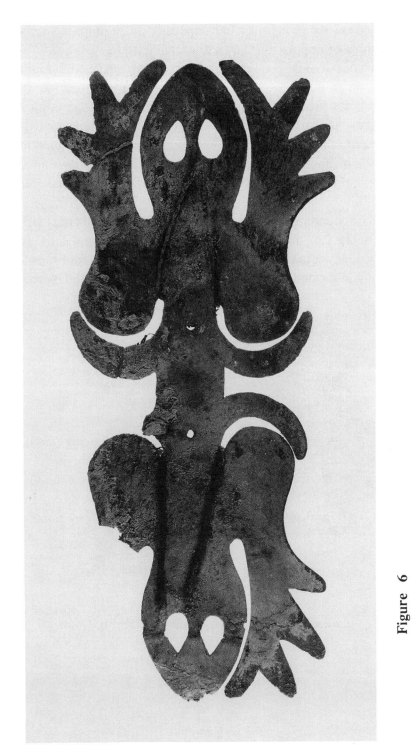

Figure 6   The Rutledge double-headed effigy is made of copper and demonstrates the artistic and technical capabilities of the Early and Middle Woodland Native Americans.

terraces in the stream valleys. The wide terraces in the central portion of the drainage also were utilized extensively for mound construction. However, the flatter rolling terrain in the western portion of the drainage was seldom used as a location for mound construction, perhaps reflecting the concentrations of populations and settlement patterns.

The purpose of most, though not all, mounds in the Licking region was to house human burials. In this sense, mounds functioned like the cemeteries and burial grounds of European and Euro-American traditions though they grew upward instead of outward as is the practice with modern cemeteries. Many burials in mounds were accompanied by beautifully made artifacts or grave goods that often are the only sources of information remaining from plundered or destroyed mound sites (figure 7).

Even the mounds which did not contain actual burials may have been used in funerary or mortuary practices. One such mound is the so-called Eagle Mound, actually a conglomeration of three or four closely associated mounds located within the Fairgrounds Circle at the Newark

Figure 7   *Bowser*
Flint Ridge blades from the Cordray Mound, Licking County

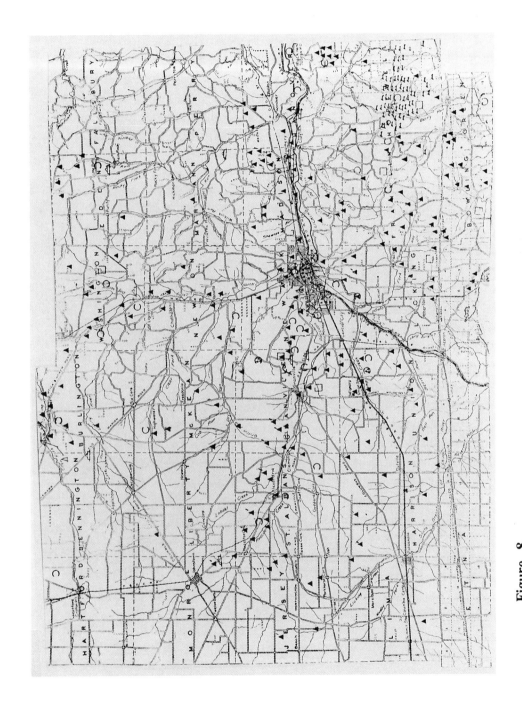

Figure 8   Mills 1914 Archaeological Atlas of Ohio

Earthworks (see Chapter five). When this mound complex was excavated in the 1920s, evidence was found of a large, multiple-room wooden structure that once stood in the place now occupied by the mound. No burials were recovered during the excavations, but a clay-lined pit in the central part of the structure was found to contain ashes and may have been a crematory basin. As a prominent part of the Newark Earthworks complex, the Eagle Mound and the Great House that it covers probably played an important role in the regional social system.

Evidence for structures have also been commonly discovered beneath singular conical mounds. Within the Licking region, the remains of single-room circular wooden structures were discovered beneath the Rutledge Mound and the Clyde Jones Mound. Some amateur and professional archaeologists have hypothesized that such structures are the remains of domestic houses. Since we now know that the mound-building peoples maintained living areas distinct from the sites of their burial mounds, a more convincing theory is that the structures figured in social and mortuary ceremonies and represent logical precursors to the kinds of structures found under large Hopewell mounds such as the Eagle Mound.

Perhaps the most unusual mound in the Licking region is an effigy mound—one built in the shape of an animal or object—located east of Granville at the spur of a ridge which juts into the Raccoon Creek valley (figures 23 & 24). The mound is known as the Alligator Mound, although even the earliest reports and descriptions of it recognized that the mound does not actually represent an alligator. The Alligator Mound, discussed in more detail in Chapter seven, has not been systematically excavated, and interpretations of its purpose vary, but evidence from other sites suggests that such effigy mounds rarely contained burials themselves though they are sometimes found in association with burial mounds.

The largest reported mound in the region, the so-called Great Stone Mound, was located one mile south of Jacksontown on a high isolated hill overlooking what is now Buckeye Lake. Constructed primarily of stone, the mound was possibly 189 feet by 207 feet at its base and 55 feet in height. According to early sources, between 10,000 and 15,000 wagon loads of stone were removed from the mound in the 1830s and used as riprap for a dike built during the construction of Buckeye Lake. Beneath the stones were 16 smaller earthen mounds, a few of which, when excavated, were said to contain human burials.

Historical sources indicate that prominent mounds were quite visible from one another. The Great Stone Mound, for example, was in sight of other large mounds in the vicinity including the still-extant Fairmount Mound (figure 9), evoking images of a complicated network of mound locations connected together by lines of sight.

The nearly complete destruction of the Great Stone Mound is but one example of the low priority given to preserving the legacy of the Moundbuilders during the past two centuries. To many early, and later, Euro-American settlers, mounds and earthworks represented an easily accessible source of building materials which could be treated almost as naturally occurring quarries. Other mounds and earthworks were leveled to prepare the ground for farming and for urban and suburban development or to ease the construction of roads, canals, and railways. Still others have been lost to the passive destruction of erosion or the active mutilations of treasure seekers. In the vast majority of cases, such destruction proceeded without study or recording keeping, leaving archaeologists the difficult task of interpreting surviving artifacts divorced from the contexts in which they were found.

Many suppositions about Moundbuilder culture have been based on the artifacts found in association with burial mounds. These grave goods further testify to the importance the Moundbuilders placed on burial and funerary practices, but they also provide evidence regarding the kinds of objects and implements the Moundbuilders used and made and the range of techniques and materials available to them. Blades made of chert or flint are among the most common artifacts, and large caches of blades have been discovered in several mounds excavated in the Licking region. Pendants, bracelets, earspools, and other objects of adornment such as gorgets also have been found in mound burials, as have beads and hammered copper plates. Several bracelets were found with burials during the excavation of the Rutledge Mound along with the effigy plate previously mentioned. Other notable artifact types are pipes, ceramics, stone tablets or abrading stones, and conical and hemispherical objects of undetermined purpose. Projectile points are also frequently found in mounds, though they often occur in the mound fill rather than specifically with burials.

Artifacts were made out of both locally available and imported raw materials, which suggests that Moundbuilders participated in trade networks to acquire materials—such as marine shell, graphite, and hematite—from quite distant regions. Mica, imported from eastern Tennessee or western North Carolina, occurred in both cut or uncut form. Copper came from the northern Great Lakes region. Flint, specifically from Flint Ridge in southeastern Licking County (figure 7), is the most commonly seen of locally available materials. Flint identifiable from Flint Ridge also has been found in sites from other areas such as Ross County in the Scioto River basin, evidencing the reciprocal nature of the trade networks in which the people of the Licking region participated.

Earthworks

Amateurs and professionals alike long have recognized distinctions between mounds and earthworks, using the latter term to describe prehistoric embankments that enclose specific areas of ground. Enclosure is another common term for such prehistoric constructions and is sometimes used synonymously with earthwork. The enclosed areas of earthworks clearly distinguish them from mounds, and major characteristics of earthworks are the shapes they enclose or define. Most often these are geometric figures. Circles are the most common earthwork form in the Licking region, but ellipses, rectangles, other shapes also occur, among them the octagon that is part of the Newark Earthworks complex(figure 10). In addition to such geometric enclosures, another kind of earthwork found in the region was designed to follow the topography.

Mills' 1914 atlas listed 36 earthworks in Licking County, counting the Newark Earthworks, which has a number of separate components, as one complex. Recent research has verified locations for 22 earthworks or earthwork groups, most of which have been resurveyed using modern equipment. All of the earthworks in the Licking region were located within the confines of Licking County with the exception of the Larimore

Figure 9   **The Fairmount Mound is one of two large burial mounds remaining in Licking County. Evidence indicates that the upper portion of the mound dates to the Middle Woodland period.**

Bowser

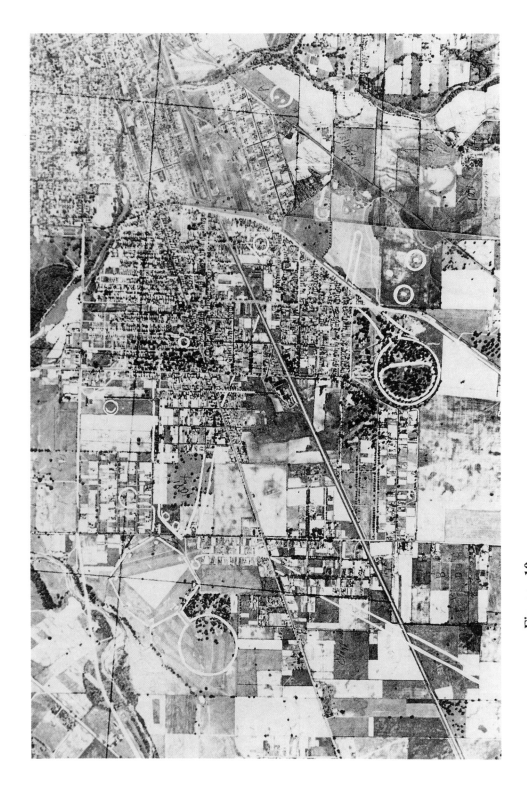

Figure 10   This 1930 aerial photograph shows the location of some of the parallel embankments associated with the Newark Earthworks.

Group, a complex of earthworks and mounds located near the small town of Lock in Knox County.

A majority (18 out of 22) of the earthworks in the Licking region were located in upland contexts, with several of these being circles that enclose individual burial mounds. The Larimore Group, for example, included a circle enclosing three acres in the valley and five small circular earthworks enclosing single mounds along with six individual unenclosed mounds—all located on upland bluffs lining the valley of the Licking River's North Fork. A trapezoidal-shaped stone enclosure on Flint Ridge, one of the more unusual embankments in the region, also surrounded an individual mound, known as the Hazlett Mound. Four other geometric enclosures located in upland contexts were small circles that do not enclose mounds. The five topographical earthworks in the region also are were located in upland contexts, most on high isolated hills. Four of these five structures also enclosed burial mounds.

Significantly, the largest and most intricate of the earthworks tend to be found in the stream valleys. Of the four earthworks located in valley contexts, only one is a small embankment associated with a single mound. The other three represent substantial geometric enclosures: the multipart complexes of the Newark Earthworks, the Granville Circle formerly located east of Granville below the Alligator mound, and the Larimore Group.

No extensive earthwork excavations have been carried out in the region. Early in the century, Mills excavated the Hazlett Mound on Flint Ridge (interpreting it as a classic Hopewell construction though, like the Rutledge Mound, atypically located in an upland context), but he basically ignored the earthwork during his investigations. Excavations at the Newark Earthworks similarly have concentrated on mounds, such as the Eagle Mound, rather than on either the earthwork structures or the general areas they enclose. Several components of the complex have been the subject of modern reconstruction and landscaping efforts, but archaeological investigations did not accompany these endeavors. The sheer volume of work involved with excavating an earthwork probably deters such investigations, although elsewhere in Ohio other earthworks have recently been excavated with promising results.

In the absence of the information careful excavations might provide, it is difficult to theorize with certainty about the techniques used in building the earthworks, the amount of time involved in their construction, or the roles they played in Moundbuilder culture. Such earthworks almost certainly were focal points for some activities of the people who built them, but the specific functions or purposes they fulfilled are less clearly understood. Early scholars often interpreted earthworks, and the topographic constructions in particular, as fortifications or other kinds of defensive structures. The larger complexes were sometimes popularly called towns or cities, implying that they were settlements. However, these assertions generally have been dismissed by modern archaeologists. Instead, most contemporary scholars believe that the earthworks were intended to designate and set aside areas where ceremonies or other specialized activities took place. The earthworks enclosing individual burial mounds probably were closely associated with burial rituals and other funerary practices, with their main or only functions directly related to the mounds they enclosed. Other earthworks might have defined other kinds of specialized sacred precincts, and large complexes such as the Newark Earthworks might have served a number of purposes.

It is interesting to note, for example, that not all the segments of the Newark Earthworks appear to have contained burial mounds. The main burial ground within the complex seems to have been the large elliptical-shaped enclosure on the eastern edge of the complex (figures 5 and 11). This segment enclosed at least a dozen mounds, including one (now destroyed) with an elaborate mica burial. The configuration and function of this enclosure might be considered analogous to the Mound City enclosure in Ross County, which also formed part of a larger complex of geometrically shaped earthworks.

Two archaeologists working together, Stuart Streuver and Gail Houart recently have suggested that Ohio earthworks were ceremonial and trading centers for an exchange network that linked much of the eastern United States into what they call the "Hopewell Interaction Sphere." Through this exchange network, prehistoric people were able to move exotic goods within and between the regions that participated in Hopewellian cultural traditions. Streuver and Houart theorize that the

Newark Earthworks in particular were a central hub for the trade of Flint Ridge chert. Streuver and Houart's ideas are not universally accepted, however, and scholars have legitimately questioned some aspects of their interpretations. Nevertheless, such complexes as the Newark Earthworks doubtless fulfilled some regional social functions, perhaps organizing and centralizing activities including, but not necessarily limited to, the funerary practices and ceremonies of participating groups.

SUMMARY AND CONCLUSIONS

During the Early and Middle Woodland periods, the Licking River basin was one of several population centers for cultural groups whose shared lifeways included the practice of building mounds and earthworks. During the latter part of the Early Woodland period, people participating in the Adena ideological system were responsible for the first mounds and earthworks in the Licking region. The local Adena groups were not complexly organized or centralized, and they probably lived in small dispersed social groups occupying well-defined social territories. The mounds they built, usually single and isolated, served as burial grounds, as markers of group affiliation to a territory, and as important locations for the social interactions of the group, partially achieved through the ceremonies associated with burials.

The earlier patterns associated with the Adena tradition were joined by Hopewell cultural traditions about 100 B.C., a date that marks the start of the Middle Woodland period. In addition to dispersed single mounds, centralized earthwork complexes also began to appear in the Licking region, probably in response to changes in the ways ritual and social interactions were organized. However, settlements of the period continued to be the farmsteads or hamlets of small household groups as was the pattern of the Early Woodland period, not larger centralized villages. These farmsteads, discussed in more detail in chapters four and six, produced a variety of foods and were dispersed throughout the environs of the earthwork complexes.

Two issues have become increasingly clear from recent research in Early and Middle Woodland period archaeology. First, the emphasis on mound and burial excavations has severely limited the scope of our understanding of the Moundbuilders. This is especially true of the Early Woodland period, but is also true for the Middle Woodland. Investigations of domestic habitation sites, in particular, are needed to develop a fuller and more accurate picture of regional social organization among the mound-building peoples. By providing new information and insights into Moundbuilder lifeways, investigations such as those at the Murphy Site already have begun to change and challenge past assumptions about prehistoric societies. Continued research of this kind can only enhance our ability to interpret the complete legacy of the Moundbuilders.

Second, the ancient monuments that do remain are in dire need of preservation. Nearly half of the once-documented mounds and earthworks have disappeared over the last century. The extensive practice of looting mounds and the consequent lack of information also offer a sad commentary on the value our society places on prehistoric remains. Preservation of any remaining unexcavated mounds and of earthworks should be a top priority for the future. A viable and workable preservation program is required to insure that the products of the Moundbuilders will be saved for future generations. Public support and interest must surely form the backbone of the preservation movement.

Figure 11   *Bowser*
      A section of the Newark Earthworks known as the Cherry
Valley Mounds is shown. The sacred burial grounds of the Hopewell
have been replaced by factories, warehouses, roads, and residences.

CHAPTER IV
THE MURPHY SITE

Willam S. Dancey

The burial mounds and geometric earthworks constructed by the Middle Woodland period occupants of the middle Ohio valley have been known for over two hundred years. Unexplored until recently, and incompletely researched even today, are the habitations and work places of these people, often referred to as the Hopewell. Despite a fairly rich picture of their ceremonial and mortuary practices, very little is known about other lifeways of these prehistoric societies. What were their settlements like? How large were they? How many people lived in them? What were their houses and other facilities like? How closely spaced were neighboring settlements? What activities took place in the settlements? What kinds of tools were used? What did the people eat and how were foods prepared? What relationships did people of neighboring regions have with one another?

Excavations of a domestic habitation site conducted between 1983 and 1987 by the Licking County Archaeology and Landmarks Society and The Ohio State University Department of Anthropology mark a beginning in the search for answers to these and other questions about Middle Woodland society in the Licking County region. This site is located on agricultural land belonging to Herb and Frank Murphy two miles east of Granville on a faint ground swell adjacent to a spring emanating from the north wall of Raccoon Creek valley. Identified by the name of the property owners, the Murphy Site is to date the most thoroughly explored site of its kind in the entire middle Ohio valley.

The Murphy Site (figure 12) initially revealed its archaeological significance through the presence of a light scattering of flint chips, by-products of stone-tool manufacturing, on the ground surface. Within the plow zone (the top layers of soil, extending to the depth affected by years of plowing) and under it in the undisturbed subsoil, the excavation produced evidence of more flint flakes, cores, and flint tools along with the trash-filled remains of cooking pits, post holes, and other facilities and structures—all concentrated within an area no larger than 250 feet

Bowser

Figure 12   The Murphy Site was occupied during the first half of the Middle Woodland period (90 BC - 200 AD). The site represents the most thoroughly investigated Middle Woodland occupational site in Ohio.

square. Pieced together, the results of the archaeological investigations at the Murphy Site provide a picture of what appears to have been a typical domestic settlement, a type of homestead in which most Middle Woodland people probably lived. Radiocarbon dates tell us that the settlement was used between approximately 100 B.C. and A.D. 200.

Investigation of the Murphy Site proceeded in a systematic fashion, employing standard approaches of archaeological field research. The objective from the beginning was to obtain comprehensive records of the layout of the settlement. Initial work concentrated on obtaining a collection of cultural items that were exposed on the surface within a grid framework. Subsequently, one-meter-square test pits were excavated at regular intervals across the site; post-hole diggers were also used to acquire samples of artifacts from the plow zone. The sediments from test pits and post holes were passed through screens to recover all cultural material for counting, weighing, and laboratory study. The use of the grid

Figure 13   *Bowser*
Feature 167 at the Murphy Site, Granville, Ohio

framework and the regular spacing of the test pits aided in detecting patterns in the distribution of different kinds of cultural fragments.

Periodically, after samples had been obtained by surface collecting and testing, heavy machinery was brought in to remove the plow zone over large areas. By the end of the four seasons of work, almost all of the settlement area was exposed. The purpose of stripping the plow zone was to expose the unplowed subsurface so that traces of prehistoric cultural features that extended deeper than the bottom of the plow zone could be detected, if present. Numerous dark stains were located and excavated completely by a process known as quartering (figure 13). After eliminating extraneous soil disturbances, such as ground hog burrows, modern fence-post molds, and root imprints, approximately 40 of the stains were found to be traces of the prehistoric occupation.

Many of these prehistoric cultural features have been tentatively identified: two as hearths, nine as earth ovens, and seven as general purpose basins. Another 18 appear to have been post molds, indicating the location of the structural elements supporting shelters. Many of the features had been filled with trash during or at the end of the site's occupation and were found to contain potsherds (broken fragments of ceramic vessels), flint debris and broken tools similar to those found on the surface and in the plow zone, fragments of cut mica, and carbonized (burned) remains of trees and other plants that had been used as fuel, construction material, and food. The fill from each feature was carefully investigated—using dry or wet screening or a floating process—in order to isolate and recover inorganic cultural artifacts such as tool fragments and organic materials such as plant parts.

The artifacts found at the Murphy Site provide significant evidence of a flint-knapping industry. Shaping flint by knapping, or chipping off flakes, the occupants of the site created razor-sharp, parallel-sided bladelets and bifacially flaked, symmetrically shaped implements such as projectile points and knives. Pottery finds indicate that the most common vessels were large, open-mouthed jars with smooth, undecorated surfaces (figure 14). Whether these were used for cooking, storage, or serving functions is not yet known. The artifacts are of types known to fall within the Middle Woodland period. With a few exceptions the flint and ceramic artifacts were made of locally available materials. The exceptions include several samples of a kind of flint found only in southern Indiana, several ceramic sherds which have paste and surface characteristics found most commonly in the southern Appalachian plateau, and scraps of mica from western North Carolina.

The archaeobotanical materials, or plant remains, recovered from the cultural features include seeds and nuts of plants that occur in the wild and some that were apparently domesticated. (Chapter six offers a more complete discussion and interpretation of such evidence from the Murphy Site.) Among the plants that seem to have been domesticated are maygrass, sunflower, erect knotweed, goosefoot (figure 15), and other edible plants which exist today largely as nuisance weeds. Significantly, no traces of maize (corn), beans, or other imported tropical cultigens were found. These tropical cultigens were central to the diet and agricultural economics of prehistoric societies in the middle Ohio valley after approximately 1000.

A map of the distribution of the cultural features (figure 16) shows an interpretation derived from pattern s observed in the different types of features combined with data based on the distribution of chipped stone materials. According to this interpretation, the settlement appears to have consisted of four zones. A "structure zone" includes the area where post molds and hearth features were found: presumably this is where houses, along with other structures, once stood. Parallel to this is the "food-preparation zone," a linear distribution of the earth ovens and basin-shaped pits. On the opposite side of the structure is an "open yard" where a small quantity of tiny flint flakes and broken tools were found. This may be where most daily activity took place (in the part of the settlement facing the central part of the valley). On a slope along the northeastern margin of the settlement is the "refuse zone." This appears to have been the area where debris from manufacturing and probably refuse of other kinds was dumped.

Understanding of regional Hopewellian societies has long been limited by the absence of concrete archaeological data, such as that obtained from the Murphy Site, regarding settlement and daily living patterns. As a result, interpretations have been based primarily on speculative assumptions and expectations. For example, scholars have

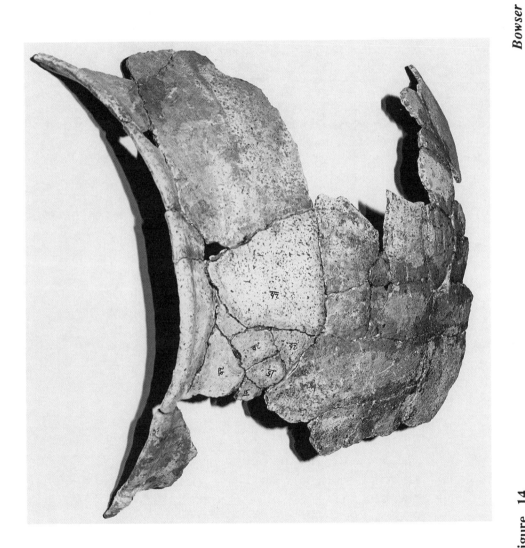

Bowser

Figure 14   Pottery from the Murphy Site provided important information about ceramic use and technology during the Middle Woodland period in Ohio

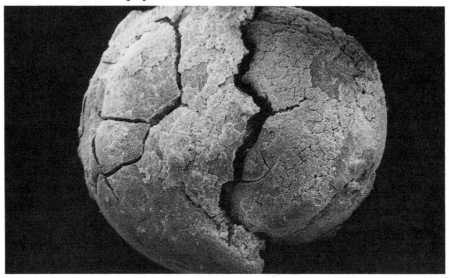

Figure 15   Scanning electron microscope photograph of Goose-foot seed from the Newark Campus (OSUN/COTC) site.

theorized that Hopewell society must have been based on multiple-household villages with a productive form of maize agriculture. One reason the excavations at the Murphy Site have proved so fascinating is that the archaeological evidence uncovered there appears to contradict such long-held, if unsubstantiated, beliefs.

Analysis of the cultural data from the Murphy Site is not yet complete but does offer tentative new interpretations of some facets of life among Middle Woodland human groups in the Licking region. Perhaps most significantly, the evidence of the Murphy Site suggests that the members of a community lived in small dispersed hamlets, or homesteads, scattered widely across the landscape rather than in large villages. Each settlement may have been occupied by a single nuclear- or extended-family unit forming a small group of not more than 25 individuals. These settlements probably consisted of one or two houses made of pole construction and accompanied by wind breaks, drying racks, and other above-ground facilities. Cooking appears to have been done in the open behind these structures, and refuse of various kinds, including chipped stone debris from manufacturing, was discarded at the edge of the settlement. Foods were acquired from local sources and mostly included species which reproduced and ripened by natural means. Domesticated plants also played a role in the diet and may have been planted and tended in small gardens adjacent to the hamlets. These plants were of local origin, however, and did not include imported tropical cultigens. Residents may have remained at the site year round and for several generations.

If the settlement pattern of Middle Woodland populations in Licking County was one of dispersed, permanent, sedentary hamlets, as described above, the earthworks might be viewed as prehistoric "community centers" where related families congregated periodically for rituals and other social activities. Burial mounds, located in the earthwork precincts and interspersed between homesteads, also may have been shared by related families. Social relationships between the closely spaced hamlets promoted the exchange and trading of exotic materials and artifacts over large areas. The question of whether significant differences in wealth, status, and power existed between families—one common interpretation of the frequently lavish nature of burial contents—cannot be resolved at present through the settlement data. Answers to this and related questions await comprehensive examination of settlements in and around the earthworks and in different habitats throughout the region. By putting evidence from burial sites in the context of other ceremonial sites, habitation sites, and other specialized kinds of sites, archaeologists may eventually develop a much fuller picture of the Hopewell world, and it is possible that the age-old "mystery of the Moundbuilders" may finally be solved.

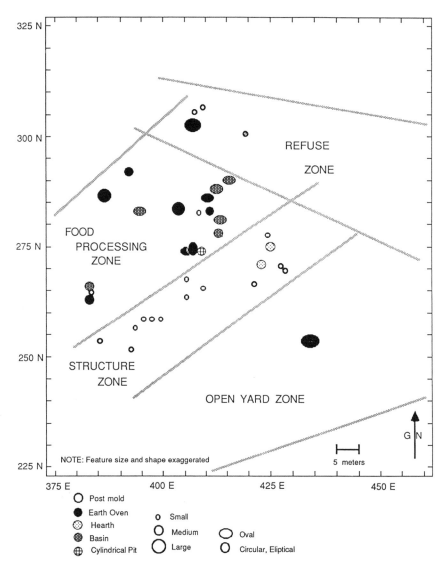

Figure 16   *Dancey*

Featuare map from the Murphy Site

CHAPTER V
THE NEWARK EARTHWORKS

Bradley T. Lepper

> ... are they here,
> the dead of other days? and did the dust
> of these fair solitudes once stir with life
> and burn with passion? Let the mighty mounds
> That overlook the rivers, or that rise
> In the dim forest crowded with old oaks,
> Answer...

With these words William Cullen Bryant vividly expressed the fascination long felt by visitors to the mounds and earthworks of eastern North America. Who built them? And for what purpose?

The largest and perhaps the most mysterious of the great geometric earthwork complexes was located in the Licking River valley, on land today in Newark, Ohio. Indeed, the Newark Earthworks was the largest complex of geometric earthworks built anywhere in the world. One author estimates that nearly seven million cubic feet of earth were gathered, basket-full by basket-full, to construct the giant circles and squares and the great octagon of prehistoric Newark. But the questions remain, questions which have been asked since early Euro-American pioneers first encountered the geometric earthen walls.

The earliest historically documented "discovery" of the Newark Earthworks by Euro-American settlers took place in 1800. According to Isaac Smucker, an early Licking County historian, Isaac Stadden stumbled across the earthworks in the autumn of that year while deer hunting. But documented study of the Newark Earthworks complex did not begin until 1820, when Caleb Atwater published his map of this enormous set of earthworks (figure 17).

Atwater believed that earthworks, such as those at Newark, were some kind of prehistoric forts and his rather schematic representation exaggerates fort-like aspects of the site while eliminating features not consistent with this interpretation. Many people still believe the earthen enclosures at Newark were ancient forts , in spite of the fact that the Great Circle at Moundbuilders State Memorial has a ditch or moat inside its formidable walls! However, professional soldiers, even in Atwater's day, recognized that such structures would make a sorry fortification. General William Henry Harrison, the hero of Tippecanoe, wrote in 1839 that the great geometric earthworks at Newark "were never intended for military defenses".

Although the earthworks were of great interest to a small number of historians and archaeologists, the majority of Newark's early settlers simply saw the monuments as obstructions in the way of the kinds of development they sought. The construction of the Ohio Canal cut through the eastern portion of the earthworks in 1827. At least one burial mound near Lock No. 7 was destroyed. The early county histories record that the mound contained numerous skeletons accompanied by abundant copper and mica artifacts. One skeleton in particular was covered with large sheets of mica.

The first scientific excavations of the Newark Earthworks were undertaken on the Fourth of July in 1836 by the Calliopean Society of the Granville Literary and Theological Institution (now Denison University). These excavations explored the so-called "observatory" at the extreme southwestern end of the circle and octagon at what is now Octagon State Memorial.(figure 21) The excavations discovered no bones or artifacts, but they did uncover a stone pavement which lay beneath the mound.

In the following years Charles Whittlesey, Ephraim G. Squier, and Edwin H. Davis began their investigations of the Newark Earthworks culminating in the publication of their detailed map of the earthworks by the Smithsonian Institution(figure 18). A cast-bronze replica of their plan , the most famous map of the Newark Earthworks, may be viewed at Moundbuilders State Memorial in front of the Ohio Indian Art Museum. In discussing the Newark complex, Squier and Davis poignantly described the continuing destruction of the site by reckless urban development which had proceeded virtually in the wake of their survey: "The ancient lines can now be traced only at intervals, among gardens and outhouses...".

Nevertheless, the wholesale destruction of the Newark Earth-

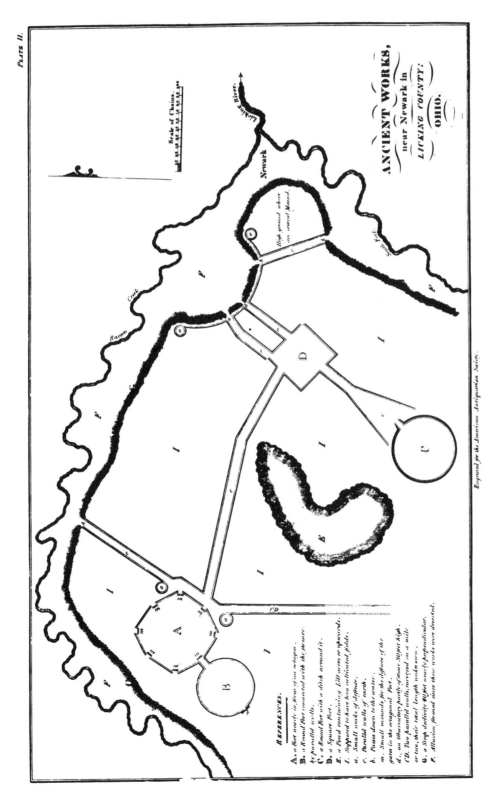

Figure 17

Caleb Atwater's map of the Newark Earthworks, 1820

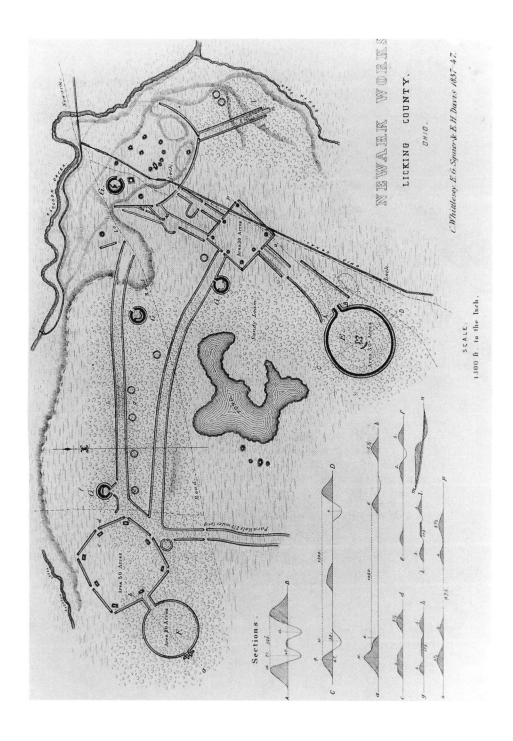

Figure 18   Squier and Davis map of The Newark Earthworks - 1848

works continued. Between 1852 and 1855 the Central Ohio Railroad was constructed through Newark. A whole series of burial mounds were leveled in order to supply earth for constructing the railroad embankment. Any bones and artifacts these mounds contained may have been carried off as curiosities, or they simply may have been shoveled into the railroad embankment.

David Wyrick, for a time Licking County's official surveyor, produced a wonderfully detailed map of the Newark Earthworks (see figure 5). Unfortunately Wyrick's genuine contributions to archaeology have been largely ignored due to the prominent part he played in the Newark "Holy Stones" fraud. (see chapter VII).

Although large portions of the Newark Earthworks have been entirely obliterated, two spectacular remnants survive as mute testimony to the monumental achievement of the Hopewell people: the Great Circle and the Observatory Circle and Octagon. These sites are now under the protection of the Ohio Historical Society, but they achieved this status through very circuitous routes. In 1892 the City of Newark purchased the Observatory Circle and Octagon and deeded the land to the State of Ohio for the encampment grounds of the Ohio National Guard. Between 1893 and 1896 the National Guard worked to restore the Octagon complex to a semblance of its former glory, then abandoned the site in 1908. The property was subsequently deeded to the Newark Board of Trade, which leased it to Moundbuilders Country Club in 1910. That June the country club's golf course officially opened, with holes designed on, around, and among the earthworks. In 1933 the Common Pleas Court of Newark ordered that the Observatory Circle and Octagon be deeded to the Ohio State Archaeological and Historical Society so that the site could be preserved as an archaeological park. Since then the site has been operated jointly as a public historical monument and a private country club.

In the early years of the twentieth century the use of this archaeological site as a golf course was seen as a unique way of preserving the mounds and earthworks while providing an important recreational facility for the community. Unfortunately, various construction activities undertaken by the country club, for example the excavation of water lines and sand traps within the enclosures, undoubtedly have destroyed evidence of what took place at this sacred site nearly twenty centuries ago.

The other major surviving segment of the Newark Earthworks, that which now comprises Moundbuilders State Memorial, fared little better. In 1853 the Great Circle was purchased by the Licking County Agricultural Society, which intended to establish the property as a prehistoric monument as well as a public recreational area. By 1854 the park had become large enough and celebrated enough to host the Ohio State Fair, and it regularly hosted the county fair, leading to its popular designation as the Fairground Circle (figure 19). In 1896 the Licking County Fairground became the site of Idewilde Park (figure 20), a kind of Disneyland of Gay Nineties Ohio. The attractions offered at this amusement park were unsurpassed in their day. They included a horse-racing track, casino, dance pavilion, billiard hall, hotel, and "European" restaurant. But the centerpiece of the park, the "crowning glory of Idewilde," was the Fairground Circle.

The Great Circle was deeded to the county in 1927 and turned over to the Ohio Historical Society by the Licking County Commissioners in 1933. Archaeologists from the Society had begun to undertake scientific explorations of the Newark Earthworks in 1928. In the summer of that year Emerson Greenman conducted excavation of the Eagle Mound located in the Great Circle. By this time archaeologists were beginning to understand something about the people who built Ohio's mounds and earthworks. The large geometric enclosures, such as the Newark Earthworks, were attributed to the prehistoric people known as the Hopewell.

Greenman discovered that the Eagle Mound was built over the site of a great longhouse of the Hopewell people. This house was almost certainly a religious or ritual site, a Hopewell equivalent of a temple or church, which may have been a charnel house where the honored dead of Hopewell society were ceremonially cremated. It was also probably an important social center for the Moundbuilders of the Licking region.

Important discoveries continue to be made at Newark. From October 1977 to January 1980 a series of archaeological investigations were conducted along the then proposed corridor for the construction of the State Route 79 Newark Expressway. This construction proceded through the heart of Newark and across what originally comprised the eastern portion of the Newark Earthworks. This area had been disturbed

Figure 19   Fairgrounds Circle, The Newark Earthworks - 1985   *Bowser*

Chance Brockway Collection

Figure   20   From 1853-1930   The Great Circle was used as the County Fairgrounds and was also known as Idlewilde Park.

extensively by previous constr" ction and development. Nevertheless, the archaeological investigations required by federal law demonstrated that important prehistoric sites had been preserved beneath the badly disturbed surface. Traces of a large square structure were discovered along with several hearths, a storage pit, and a large refuse pit. This site may have been a mortuary camp where skilled artisans manufactured ceremonial objects for inclusion in the nearby burial mounds. On the other hand, it may simply represent a small living site like the Murphy Site (see chapter IV).

Much of the Newark Earthworks complex has been destroyed. Little now remains for archaeologists to study in their search for answers to our many questions about this wonderful site. But even though we can't say exactly why these magnificent earthen lines were designed and built, we *can*, with some certainty, refute some common misconceptions.

The Newark Earthworks was not a fortress, nor a city, nor merely a cemetery. Instead it must have served some combination of functions. It appears to have been a prehistoric American ceremonial center combining aspects of Egypt's pyramids, England's Stonehenge, and France's Chartres Cathedral. But why was this vast center of the Moundbuilders located in Licking County?

The rugged hills barely ten miles southwest of Newark are capped with rich deposits of brilliantly colored chert or flint. Flint from Flint Ridge was a highly prized commodity within the trading network of Hopewell society. It is surely no coincidence that the largest complex of Hopewellian earthworks was constructed on the closest available land surface to this important resource. Indeed, it is likely that one function which the earthworks served was that of a trading center where artifacts crafted from Flint Ridge flint were brought and exchanged for copper ornaments from the Great Lakes, mica cut-outs from the Carolinas, and possibly even obsidian tools from the Rocky Mountains. So it is not entirely facetious to suggest that the Newark Earthworks were the original "Indian Mound Mall."

Bowser

Figure 21   Octagon State Memorial, part of the Newark Earthwork Complex is a site operated by The Ohio Historical Society.

CHAPTER VI
LICKING COUNTY'S FIRST FARMERS

Paul E. Hooge and DeeAnne Wymer

One of the primary areas of research by the Licking County Archaeology and Landmarks Society over the past seven years has been the study of how farming evolved among the county's first inhabitants. Much of this research has focused on the Murphy Sites located along Newark-Granville Road. (The Murphy Site discussed in chapter four is only one of several sites that have been excavated and studied on the Murphy's property.) Significant information also has been recovered from the Nu-Way site on Waterworks Road and from behind Adena Hall on the grounds of The Ohio State University–Newark.

The years of painstaking, even tedious, excavation and analysis have paid off, and we can now begin to tell the story of how hunting and gathering populations in the area began to adopt simple but effective gardening methods about three thousand years ago and, eventually, developed into sophisticated farmers by about one thousand years ago.

The oldest evidence of agriculture in the Americas is from Mexico, Central America, and Peru. In excavations at Peruvian dry rock shelters, domesticated squash has been found preserved in levels that can be dated to nine thousand years ago. By four thousand years ago Central Americans had become established farmers, while the residents of eastern North America were just beginning to become efficient gardeners. The archaeological record of this time in the Midwest shows that some plants were changing in ways that indicate domestication.

In an educational video about Ohio prehistory produced about fifteen years ago and still used in many schools, the commentator states in the opening line, "a warm place to sleep by the fire, a few chunks of deer meat, and a little shelter from the cold winter wind, that's about all early people who lived in this land we call Ohio had." We now know that this rather austere picture was not accurate in the least. A brief inventory of available food resources in the prehistoric Ohio environment should leave no doubt that Native Americans were never restricted to a diet of a "few chunks of deer meat."

The quality of life enjoyed by Native Americans certainly was enhanced by an environment rich in edible plants and animals. The people of the Archaic period (6000-1000 B.C.) adapted quickly to the environmental changes that ended the Ice Age and continued to be extremely efficient hunters and gatherers in the predominantly forest environment of central Ohio. The white-tailed deer was a primary source of protein for Native Americans, but many other sources of red meat were also available. Elk, possibly forest bison, mountain lion, lynx, beaver, wolverine, black bear, red wolf, gray wolf, porcupine, raccoon, red fox, coyote, muskrat, gray squirrel, fox squirrel, woodchuck, eastern cottontail, and opossum—any or all of these animals might also have figured in the diet of the early Native Americans. Birds were another valuable food resource. Because of their size and abundance, passenger pigeons, wild turkeys, and several species of waterfowl were probably among the most important birds included in the Native American diet. We cannot be sure where central Ohio then fell on the fly-way pattern of migrating waterfowl, however it is certain there was an abundance of waterfowl in the area on at least a seasonal basis.

Nonetheless, game made up less than fifty percent of the overall caloric intake of Native Americans though it was the chief source of protein for most of prehistory. During the Archaic period in Ohio hunter-gatherers efficiently collected wild plant seeds in the forests. Nuts were extremely important and available in huge quantities in the fall. Black walnut and hickory trees were the most prevalent sources of the edible nuts, but acorn, hazelnut, and chestnut were also available. Berries and other fruit such as black cherries, black raspberries, elderberries, grapes, hawthorns, mulberries, pawpaws, viburnum, and wild plums were all important food resources. A variety of green plants, some of whose seeds were gathered, added important nutrients. Many of these plants would later be domesticated; these useful plants, mostly classified as weeds today, included maygrass, sumpweed, knotweed, and goosefoot. Other edible plants included a variety of tubers, cattail root, amaranth, and poke.

Fish and shell fish also provided nutrients for the prehistoric diet in some areas, for central Ohio abounds with streams, rivers, small lakes, and ponds. The species of fish and shellfish available for human consumption would have varied with the environment and probably differed from those in the region today. Of the more than 124 different types of river mussel, for example, that once existed in the Ohio River drainage, only a few remain. Throughout prehistory Native Americans utilized this resource in varying degrees. At some sites along major tributaries, prehistoric middens, or trash heaps, include thousands of mussel shells left by feasting natives.

As early as 7000 years ago native populations in Kentucky, Tennessee, and possibly Ohio were using a variety of weed squash, and by 4000 years ago it appears that this plant had been domesticated. This squash was perhaps the first plant grown intentionally in a controlled environment in North America. Archaeological evidence from many sites also demonstrates the importance of nut resources in the prehistoric diet, with hickory almost always the dominant type.

The Early Woodland period (1000–100 B.C.) was a time of dramatic change and experimentation for Native American populations in the Ohio valley. Trade became an important factor and opened the region to new materials and ideas. Ceremonialism, especially associated with death, became a dominant theme, evidenced by the construction of the mounds to memorialize the dead and identify the sacredness of specific spaces. Total dependency on the forest, and the natural environment in general, as a source for food ended during this period, and local populations began to develop a way of life that was in part more self-sufficient. Early in this period, if not late in the Archaic, ceramics were introduced or developed. The use of ceramics revolutionized the ways in which food could be prepared and stored, thus providing a moderately more secure lifestyle.

By 2000 years ago Native Americans in this part of North America had developed a system of gardening that was unique in the world. This system did not include maize (corn) field agriculture, but instead depended on a group of domesticated local seed plants known as the Eastern Agricultural Complex or EAC. The EAC is composed of two oily seeds—sumpweed and sunflower—and four starchy seeds: maygrass, knotweed, goosefoot, and in some areas a little barley. In addition, a hard-shelled, bitter-fleshed squash (bottle gourd) was grown.

One of the major sources for scientific information about the EAC gardening system has been based on research conducted at the Murphy Sites located just east of Granville, Ohio. The area was the scene of prehistoric habitation for perhaps 11,000 years. Work at the Murphy Sites began in 1983 at a location specifically designated Murphy Site No. 1 or 33 LI 212.

The occupants of this site, which was inhabited between about 100 B.C. and A.D. 200, probably did not find the land ready for their gardens. Instead they faced a heavily forested area along the edge of a wetland that seasonal flooding transformed into a shallow pond. Drainage from the surrounding hills as well as spring-fed streams wound through the site and settled in a natural basin before draining into Raccoon Creek. This environment was certainly attractive to the occupants, being a natural food producing area and a haven for waterfowl and a variety of other animals.

Along the edge of this natural wetland, Native Americans of the Woodland period opened up the forest, planted their crops, and built their homes. Clearing the forest so sufficient sunlight would reach the crops presented problems, but not ones that these creative and industrious people found insurmountable. These early residents probably visited the sites where they hoped to establish their new home a year or two before actually settling them. On such preliminary visits they would remove the outer bark from trees, a procedure (called girdling) that causes the trees to die. This could easily be accomplished with stone axes and other tools. Once the trees had died, the forest would be open to sunlight. The dead trees could then be felled, if desired, by a combination of burning and chopping at the base of the tree, in order to expose more land for gardens.

With new rich soil exposed and plenty of sunlight, gardens could be defined, prepared, and planted with Eastern Agricultural Complex crops. When ready for harvesting, pods from both the oily sumpweed and sunflower could be dried and the seeds removed. The starchy members of the EAC (goosefoot, maygrass, knotweed) have compact seed heads that contain thousands of small seeds, not unlike sesame or poppy seeds. These crops could be harvested by stripping the seeds off the plant. Seed heads could also have been dried and stored without stripping.

Archaeologists have evidence that natives may have cleared and occupied an area and then abandoned it only to return at some point in the future. Leaving these clearings in the forest untended provided an opportunity for other plant species to fill the ecological niche. Plants such as raspberry, sumac, elderberry, and hazelnut would thrive in these open spaces. Archaeologists theorize that representative increases of raspberry, elderberry, and especially hazelnut in the archaeological record (based on the evidence offered by trash pits, cooking hearths, and other cultural features) indicate that the forest changed over time in response to human manipulations of the environment. It has also been suggested that nut production was encouraged during the Woodland period. By killing other trees surrounding a good nut-producing tree, the nut tree would expand its foliage and produce even more nuts.

With all of this in mind we have to reevaluate our antiquated and unsubstantiated vision of what prehistoric people were like. Native Americans were highly productive, thoughtful individuals. This becomes even more obvious during the Middle Woodland period (100 B.C.–A.D. 400), when Native Americans turned a considerable portion of their physical and social energy toward the construction of massive earthwork complexes.

The gardens of the Hopewell people are gone, so how do we know the carbonized seed remains found in trash pits or cooking hearths are those from domesticated plants and not simply wild plants? Research has demonstrated that sunflower and sumpweed seeds recovered from sites increase in size over time. By A.D. 200 these seeds are twice the size of wild specimens. Goosefoot also changes over time when domesticated; the seed coat becomes thinner and the overall shape of the seed changes.

The starchy seeds like maygrass and goosefoot may have been processed for consumption or storage by roasting. This technique burns off unwanted portions of the seed heads. The seeds may have been ground into flour for flatcakes or boiled into a porridge. During the Historic period (1650–1850), Wisconsin tribes are known to have processed wild rice seeds using this technique.

Archaeologists studying wood charcoal at prehistoric sites in the Midwest have noted that the percentage of charcoal from disturbed or open habitats increases with time. The most pronounced changes begin to occur in the Middle Woodland period. These changes support the theory that native populations were increasingly modifying their environment through time.

The contents of refuse pits from the Middle Woodland period excavated at the Murphy property and behind Adena Hall on the Newark Campus differ from those found at Late Woodland sites of several centuries later (A.D.400–800). Middle Woodland sites show relatively high densities of EAC seeds: the starchy seeds of the EAC make up about 75% of the identified seeds found at Murphy Site No. 1. Late Woodland sites, by contrast, often reveal significantly higher proportions of nutshell in their middens. However, local inhabitants during both periods apparently utilized diverse hunting, gathering, and gardening strategies to obtain the food they needed.

Only in the past decade and a half has an accurate picture of prehistoric food production and subsistence patterns become known. Many prominent archaeologists previously thought that the Moundbuilders of the Early and Middle Woodland periods grew corn and lived in large villages. Recent research has not substantiated these beliefs, although corn may have appeared in ceremonial contexts in a few burial mounds of the period. The late Jesse Walker, a local amateur archaeologist reported finding carbonized (burned) corn cobs in the Deeds burial mound south of Granville. There is no reason to believe his report is not accurate, but no corn has been discovered to date in systematically excavated Middle Woodland refuse pits or abandoned cooking hearths.

By the end of the Middle Woodland period in about A.D.400, however, some fundamental changes occurred among Native American populations that apparently caused them to shift from living in small hamlets of perhaps 10-30 individuals to larger and more formally structured village sites with perhaps 100-150 residents. These changes do not appear to have been caused by fluctuations in food resources or alterations in methods of food production. Instead they seem to reflect cultural changes.

So, when did corn (maize), which later became a staple food, enter the diet of Native Americans in this region? Current theory based on the archaeological record and on isotope and dental analysis of skeletal samples from the Midwest indicates that corn appears in the diet of Native Americans only after A.D.800. Prior to this time, maygrass and squash appear to have been the most prominent food crops, with collected hickory nuts, walnuts, hazelnuts, and acorns assuming increasing importance during the Late Woodland period. Between A.D.800 and 900, almost concurrently with the introduction of corn into the local Native American diet, the starchy seeds of the EAC completely disappear from the archaeological record in Ohio. Prehistoric inhabitants then put their energy into corn and squash production. By the time Columbus arrived in the Americas, the agricultural picture had become even more complex with beans as well as corn, squash, and other crops being grown.

When scholars have discussed and described the impact on Native American horticulture and agriculture on the world, attention often has been focused on tobacco and the negative ramifications of its introduction to Europe and elsewhere for world health. Ironically, tobacco has proved to be nearly as devastating, though in a slower fashion, as the diseases Europeans brought to the Americas. Concentration on the negative effects of tobacco, however, need not overshadow the many and immeasurable positive contributions of Native American horticulture and agriculture. Although some of the foods cultivated by Native American gardeners of the Woodland period have been relegated to the status of nuisance weeds, others have remained significant crops. Sunflowers, for example, might be mentioned along with corn and beans as among the numerous useful crops Native Americans introduced to European populations. At the same time, a search for still-evident contributions should not obscure understanding and appreciation of the creative approaches Woodland period gardeners brought to satisfying their own food needs.

What we can actually know about the past depends upon the time, energy, and funding we are willing to devote to it. The excavations at the Murphy Sites and the information they have provided about food procurement and production in the Middle Woodland period offer an excellent example of a project supported by volunteers as well as donations from the community. These projects also demonstrate how much can be learned when dedicated local amateurs work with professional archaeologists to solve difficult research problems, such as those involved in understanding the emergence of Licking County's first farmers.

CHAPTER VII

JUST HOW HOLY ARE THE NEWARK "HOLY STONES?"

Bradley T. Lepper

The spectacular mound and earthwork sites of eastern North America once were thought to be the work of a lost race of white-skinned "Moundbuilders." According to proponents of this now-discarded theory, the Native Americans were considered too unsophisticated to have accomplished such astonishing engineering feats. The racist overtones of such beliefs are echoed in the perennial chorus of claims purporting to "prove" that one or another Old World civilization discovered and colonized the Americas long before Leif Ericksson and Christopher Columbus.

One of the more persistent contenders for the leading role in this hypothetical drama has been the so-called Lost Tribes of Israel, and a handful of graven images from Licking County, Ohio, has been offered as evidence for a prehistoric Hebrew presence in America. These objects, popularly known as the Newark "Holy Stones" (figure 22), are stone carvings of diverse form engraved with Hebrew writing. These peculiar artifacts were said to have been found within prehistoric Indian mounds in and around Newark. This is a remarkable claim because, if true, such discoveries would lend credence to the notion that the prehistoric mounds and earthworks of eastern North America were indeed built by the Lost Tribes of Israel—or at least that seafaring Hebrews made their way into central Ohio long before Columbus "discovered" America.

Although the Newark "Holy Stones" have long been dismissed as frauds by archaeologists, the controversy has been resurrected in recent years by several individuals with an apparent interest in prehistory, but no formal training in archaeology. Foremost among these authors is Robert Alrutz, a retired professor of biology at Denison University. Alrutz claims that professional archaeologists have rejected the "Holy Stones" as frauds because professional archaeologists are scientific bigots with closed minds. On the other hand, Alrutz believes that individuals such as himself, whose interest in the "Holy Stones" is untrammeled by academic training in archaeology, "are more receptive to varied interpretations of evidence."

Certainly persons uneducated in a given discipline may be more willing to accept a variety of unusual "interpretations of evidence" in that field. For example, individuals with no background in physics or astronomy may be willing to accept the evidence of their senses that the earth is stationary and the sun revolves around it. Some may even be persuaded to accept the idea that the sun is a fiery chariot driven by God.

But Professor Alrutz is wrong about archaeologists. Although professional archaeologists do indeed approach subjects such as the Newark "Holy Stones," with an "inherent skepticism," Alrutz is sadly mistaken when he equates proper skepticism with unthinking bigotry. When someone claims to have seen a rabbit in their garden, there is no reason to doubt them. But if the same person says they saw a unicorn in their garden, a reasonable person might ask to see some proof of this extraordinary claim. Likewise, Newark's "Holy Stones" have such extraordinary implications for New World prehistory that the burden of "proof" must be on those who would have us accept such a radical view of the past.

Modern scientific archaeology has achieved a rich and detailed understanding of the development of Native American cultures. Accepting the validity of the Newark "Holy Stones" means overturning much of what scholars have learned about ancient America over the last century and a half. Some day, new evidence may radically change our understanding of particular aspects of American prehistory, but archaeologists are completely justified in expecting an extraordinary level of proof for a claim with such extraordinary consequences.

This brief article is concerned with answering a simple and specific question—on the basis of what is known about these artifacts and the context of their discovery, can we accept the Newark "Holy Stones," beyond a reasonable doubt, as evidence of ancient Hebrews having lived in prehistoric Ohio?

The central figure in the Newark "Holy Stones" controversy is David Wyrick. Wyrick was a colorful, eccentric character, who lived in Newark, Ohio, during the mid-nineteenth century. He devoted much of

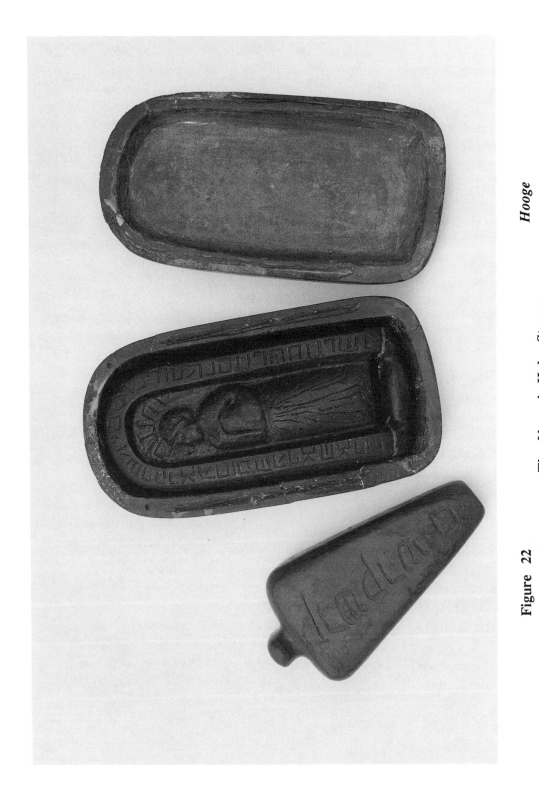

Hooge

The Newark Holy Stones

Figure 22

his energies to attempting to prove the theory that the Lost Tribes of Israel were the builders of Ohio's mounds and earthworks. This "notion" did not originate with Wyrick but had been a popular explanation for the origins of the Native American in general and the Moundbuilders in particular since the seventeenth century.

Prior to the summer of 1860 Wyrick's search for evidence supporting his theory had proven fruitless. No shred of evidence for the presence of ancient Israelites had been found among Ohio's prehistoric mounds. However, within a few short months, Wyrick triumphantly proclaimed that the "Hebrew theory" was proven by his excavation of two stone objects engraved with Hebrew writing: the "Keystone" which Wyrick and his son excavated from within a depression inside of one of Newark's small circular enclosures, and the "Decalogue Stone," a pecuilarly shaped object excavated by Wyrick and a party of men from the Great Stone Mound near Jacksontown . The "Decalogue Stone" is so named because the Ten Commandments are engraved upon its faces. Here indeed was apparent proof that Ohio's Moundbuilders had at least some contact with pre-Columbian Hebrew immigrants.

Charles Whittlesey, one of Ohio's early archaeologists, argued that these artifacts were fakes crafted by Wyrick himself. He claimed that after Wyrick's death a Hebrew bible was found among his personal effects and, for Whittlesey, this "fully cleared up the mystery of Hebrew inscriptions" in Ohio: Wyrick had simply copied the inscriptions from the Hebrew text. Jefferey Gill of Newark recently uncovered evidence that these inscriptions were copied from modern Hebrew originals by Wyrick and /or other hoaxers. The letters on the "Keystone" are thoroughly modern in character and the unique alphabet on the "Decalogue Stone" represents a creative attempt to convert modern Hebrew letters into forms which would appear archaic. Mistakes were made, however, in transcribing from modern Hebrew into the antique - looking, but fraudulent, "Decalogue Stone" alphabet.These transcription errors are the 'smoking gun' which proves that the "Decalogue Stone" is a modern forgery.

One year after Wyrick's death, the mystery of the "Holy Stones" appeared to deepen with the discovery of two more objects bearing

Hebrew inscriptions from another mound in Madison Township. But, according to Whittlesey, there was no mystery here either. John Nicol, a Newark dentist, admitted to making these artifacts and planting them in the mound as a joke. Nicol, who previously had accused Wyrick of fabricating the original "Holy Stones," decided to make his own "Hebrew" artifacts in order "to show how easily people could be deceived." Alrutz rejected Whittlesey's claim as hearsay and argued that Nicol was not capable of such a sophisticated forgery.

Huston McCulloch, Professor of Economics at The Ohio State University, recently announced in The Newark *Advocate* (6 June 1990) a new" translation" of the Hebrew inscriptions from these two artifacts that conclusively shows them to be clever hoaxes perpetrated by John Nicol. The English equivalents of the Hebrew letters, when read in proper sequence, spell out the following: J-H-NCL. By adding the vowels, which Hebrew does not supply, McCulloch derived the name J[ohn]-H-N[i]C[o]l. It seems, therefore, that the waggish Dr. Nicol signed his name on two "Un-Holy" Stones before planting them in the Madison Township mound. Unfortunately, uncritical enthusiasts, grasping at straws to prove a treasured theory, failed for more than a century to get the joke.

Alrutz insists that McCulloch's demonstration that two of the "Holy Stones" are fakes has no implications for the authenticity of Wyrick's original discoveries. McCulloch agrees. However, one important test of authenticity for the "Holy Stones" would be the discovery of similar artifacts by independent investigators. If the only corroborative discoveries are proven to be frauds, it is reasonable to suppose that the original finds are themselves fraudulent. It is important to keep an open mind, but it is also useful and legitimate to evaluate nineteenth-century claims on the basis of twentieth-century knowledge. In the case of the Newark "Holy Stones," this means that Wyrick's evidence for his claim that ancient Hebrews lived in Licking County must be balanced by the utter lack of corroborating evidence obtained by modern investigators using improved methods of survey and excavation. The Newark "Holy Stones" were "discovered" during a period when the science of archaeology was in its infancy. There were no established field techniques, and methods of recording and analyzing data were quite unsophisticated. During this period, serious consideration was being given to the notion that Native American cultures had been influenced by various Old World civilizations and there was, according to one contemporary author, virtually a "constant recurrence of frauds" in support of these competing theories. But if ancient Hebrews were present in the Americas, then we should find evidence of their settlements: towns, villages, trading camps, etc. For example, it has been shown that Vikings were present in North America before Columbus by the discovery and excavation of the site of L'Anse aux Meadows in Newfoundland.

Unfortunately for advocates of the "Holy Stones", no modern archaeological research project in the Americas has yet located an ancient Hebrew settlement. Moreover, scores of twentieth-century scientific excavations of Woodland period sites in eastern North America have not produced a single artifact derived from any Old World civilization.

It should also be pointed out that Old World colonists would (and did) carry with them much more than a few enigmatic stone carvings. After Columbus' voyage of 1492, and especially after De Soto's and Coronado's expeditions in 1539 and 1540, Native peoples in North American were decimated by European diseases against which they had no immunity. In other words, they had never been exposed to these diseases before. If they had, at some time in the past, been exposed to Hebrews, or any other Old World peoples, then the catastrophic plagues would have occurred at the time of this initial contact. Moreover, such a catastrophe would not have been repeated in the sixteenth century because the surviving Native Americans would have built up immunities to the foreign diseases.

The "Holy Stones" of Newark cannot reasonably be accepted as credible evidence for a pre-Columbian Hebrew presence in the New World. Given the unusual circumstances surrounding the discovery of the "Holy Stones" the modern character of the alphabets engraved upon them, the limitations of archaeological science at the time of their "discovery," and the complete lack of corroborating evidence, the most reasonable interpretation is that the various "Holy Stones" from Licking County are frauds perpetrated by John Nicol and others. It likely will not be possible to prove to everyone's satisfaction that these "Holy" relics are fakes. Nevertheless, there is no scientific justification for accepting these anomalous artifacts as genuine. Even if it were not so obvious that the objects were fraudulent it would not be reasonable to abandon the detailed understanding of New World prehistory achieved by modern archaeology in order to accommodate the extraordinary implications of a handful of strange relics with such an uncertain provenience.

CHAPTER VIII
THE ALLIGATOR MOUND:
A CASE STUDY OF ARCHAEOLOGY
AND
PRESERVATION IN LICKING
COUNTY

Paul E. Hooge

In 1848 Ephraim G. Squier and Edwin H. Davis published *Ancient Monuments of the Mississippi Valley*, their celebrated survey of prehistoric mounds and earthworks, as part of the series "Smithsonian Contributions to Knowledge." Among the prehistoric sites Squier and Davis described with particular attention and detail was a Licking County effigy mound known locally as the "Alligator Mound" (figure 23), located about one mile east of the center of Granville, on a hill overlooking the village and the Raccoon Creek valley. The two pioneering archaeologists considered the Alligator Mound one of the most fascinating and significant monuments they had visited, and their regard was shared by many of their contemporaries. In fact, the consensus opinion among nineteenth- and early twentieth-century scholars was that only the Great Serpent Mound in Adams County rivalled the Alligator in importance. But while Serpent Mound retained its renown into the late twentieth century, the Alligator was largely forgotten.

As a student of archaeology, I had read about the Alligator Mound in various histories and chronicles, but I had never seen it and was uncertain whether the mound still existed. In June of 1983, I decided to try to locate the Alligator. After several phone calls I discovered that the mound did indeed still exist, but no one could provide specific instructions for finding it. The mound seemed to have fallen victim to contemporary indifference and neglect.

At that time, the Licking County Archaeology and Landmarks Society (LCALS)had recently been incorporated, and we were involved in the first year of excavation at the Murphy Site on Newark-Granville Road, close to the reported location of the Alligator Mound. Several

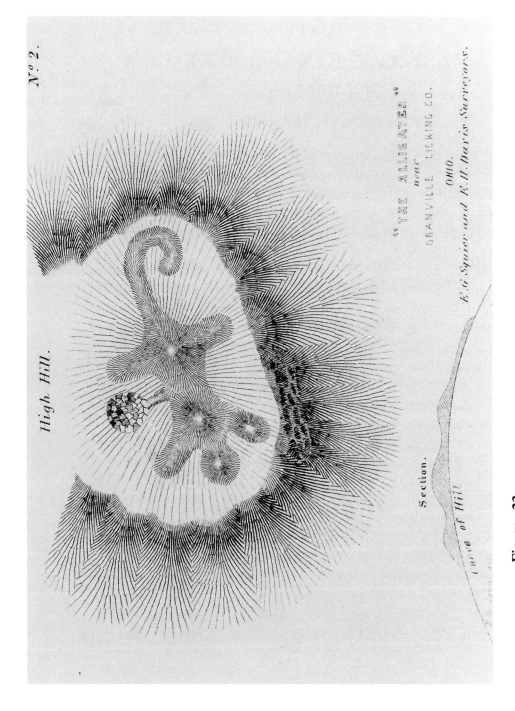

Figure 23   The Alligator Mound from Squier and Davis - 1848

members of the society accompanied me on searches for the mound, but each time we returned frustrated. One hot day in July, Richard Stallings, a local amateur archaeologist, volunteered his services at the Murphy Site. Stallings, who worked for William Wright, informed us that the mound was located on Mr. Wright's Bryn Du Farm property, only a half a mile from our excavation.

Stallings and I visited the Alligator Mound later that month. It was situated on a prominent point, just as Squier and Davis described, and I was amazed by the condition and appearance of the mound. Grazing cattle had kept the grass on the mound short, and every detail was visible. The beast's legs seemed to embrace the hill; its head faced Granville's Mount Parnassus, where a burial mound was reportedly excavated over a century ago. The tail was curled tightly and extended to the east toward a neighboring ridge where a large, heart-shaped earth enclosure with several conical mounds had once been located. I wondered if all these sites had been related in some way to the Alligator Mound.

A young hawthorn tree had sprouted at the mound's mid-section, and a groundhog had taken up residence at the high point in the hip. Several multiflora rose plants were trying to establish themselves, but generally the mound was free of the dense brush that surrounded it on three sides. The only serious obstructions to the observer were the frequent and fresh piles of cow manure.

The situation was more than somewhat astonishing. Here, in the middle of a cow pasture, was a prehistoric built site of international significance, and nothing was being done to preserve it for this and future generations. After some investigation, I realized that the vast majority of individuals living in the county had never even heard of the mound.

The size of the mound was very impressive: over 200 feet long and 100 feet wide. The extra appendage extending from the north side of the mound, which had figured prominently in the early descriptions, was still visible though considerably eroded by various forces, including curious tourists or relic hunters. The front left leg had been shortened prior to 1848 when Ashel Aylesworth, the owner of the property at that time, had been quarrying for stone. According to Squier and Davis, Aylesworth ceased his quarrying when concerned citizens in the vicinity asked him to stop.

Squier and Davis added in a footnote: "It is to be hoped that the citizens of Granville will adopt means to permanently and effectually restore it [the mound] from invasion."

Squier and Davis' words echoed in my mind on that first visit. I asked myself why, after over one hundred and thirty years, no one—including the citizens of Granville—had taken Squier and Davis' advice.

Concern about the mound's future was reflected in the writings of many authors throughout the last half of the nineteenth century. Dr. James H. Salisbury, who conducted another survey of the mound in 1862, noted that "the plow has been suffered to pass over this mysterious mound many times, consequently reducing its height which is from four to five feet." Prominent Licking County historian Isaac Smucker noted in 1875 that the mound not only suffered from the eroding effects of cultivation but also showed damage from uprooted trees that had left large holes in its surface.

Professor Frederick W. Putnam of Harvard University's Peabody Museum, the most eminent and skilled archaeologist working in Ohio during the last quarter of the nineteenth century, also urged local officials to protect the Alligator Mound and other sites. In February of 1885 Putnam wrote a letter to the then newly established Ohio State Archaeological and Historical Society (OSAHS), in which he expressed his fears regarding threats to the major prehistoric mounds and earthworks of Ohio. Concerning the Alligator, he stated: "The two famous effigy mounds of the state, the 'Serpent' and the 'Alligator' should be saved at once from further destruction...." When his advice received little or no response in Ohio, Putnam personally raised funds to preserve and study Serpent Mound from a group of concerned women in Boston. Unfortunately, preservation of the Alligator Mound was not included in Peabody's efforts.

In the same year as Peabody's letter and perhaps in response to it, the OSAHS Preservation Committee did assign an official, George Frederick Wright, to the task of evaluating the condition of the major mounds and earthworks of the state. After his inspection of the Alligator Mound, Wright wrote: "Near Granville ... the Alligator Mound is still in pretty good condition. But one of the most vivid things in my memory is the picture of the sheep, cattle, and horses which I saw stamping flies under the shade cast by a solitary tree upon the Alligator Mound. Their busy hoofs will not long suffer any remnant of it to continue visible."

These comments from Salisbury, Smucker, and Wright indicate that the Alligator Mound was under cultivation and subjected to grazing during much of the later nineteenth century. And the fears they expressed regarding the resulting erosion and other destruction were well founded. Today, the tail is extremely eroded: even though its form can be easily distinguished from the air, its end point and line of curvature are difficult to determine when attempting to observe and measure the mound from the ground.

Early scholars voiced nearly unanimous agreement regarding the mound's importance and need for preservation but found much to debate when discussing its function and seeking to identify the animal it depicts. Although the mound has long been known as the "Alligator," few authorities have accepted that this is the animal portrayed in the mound's form, and the use of this name still sparks contention. Why call it the Alligator Mound when the alligator probably had nothing to do with local prehistoric beliefs, mythology, or religion? Apparently, the mound received its name from some unknown early settler in the area who, upon seeing its resemblance to the southern reptile, dubbed the mound with the name "Alligator," and the name stuck. Squier and Davis noted: "It is known in the vicinity as 'the Alligator' which designation has been adopted for want of a better one, although the figure bears as close a resemblance to the lizard as any other reptile."

Salisbury, who produced an excellent illustration of the mound for his 1862 survey report, suggested that the mound was "undoubtedly intended to represent the panther, king of the American forest" and considered it "a good earth embossed representation" of this animal. J. W. Powell, writing in 1833, believed the mound represented an opossum, a designation also supported by Gerald Fowke in 1902. Fowke thought that an animal as unusual as the opossum would surely have been venerated by prehistoric people and that the extra appendage protruding from the right side of the mound could represent a marsupial's pouch, thus supporting identification of the animal as an opossum. A brochure distributed by the Newark Chamber of Commerce in about 1935 refers to the mound as the Raccoon or Alligator Mound.

My experience has been that there is frequently more debate concerning what to call the mound than about how to properly preserve, study, or restore it. We will probably never know what animal the mound was intended to represent, and to change its name at this point would simply apply another equally incorrect designation. Tradition refers to the mound as the "Alligator." Research and education alone will correct the misconceptions concerning the mound, its origins, and what meaning it might have had for its builders.

Although interpretations of the mound's function have varied in many specifics, almost all commentators have agreed that the mound served some type of ceremonial purpose. Squier and Davis described the unusual appendage of the mound as a graded way leading to an elevated circular space "covered with stones which have been much burned." They referred to this space as an altar and concluded: "It seems more than probable that this singular effigy, like that last described (Serpent Mound), has its origins in the superstitions of its makers. It was perhaps the high place where sacrifices were made, or stated on extraordinary occasions and where ancient people gathered to celebrate the rites of their unknown worship."

Squier and Davis' mention that the mound might have been a location for sacrifices was perhaps unfortunate, since it may have led later individuals such as Dr. Frederick Larkin (1880) and the Reverend Dr. J.P. MacLean (1879) to conclude that the site was indeed dedicated to the image of the alligator and devoted to punishment and destruction of heretics by fire—wild speculations that remain unsupported by any concrete archaeological evidence.

The meaning and use of the Alligator Mound in prehistoric times still remain mysteries. Personally, I like Salisbury's evocative concluding remarks on the mound. He wrote, "unknown centuries have passed since this symbolic pile was raised and still it keeps its faithful watch over consecrated soil (the Newark Earthworks) where repose the silent remains of one of the great central citadels of the mound builders."

The age of the mound also has been the subject of speculation, but we can make more educated guesses about age than we can about function. Current research in the county indicates that the construction of mounds for ceremonial purposes other than burial begins at about 200 B.C. Mounds of the effigy type appear later, perhaps about 2000 years ago. The practice of building effigy mounds and geometric earthworks in Ohio ends about A.D. 400. Thus the Alligator Mound is probably about 1800 years old and was probably constructed by the cultural group we refer to as Hopewell. Research conducted around the Alligator Mound by the Ohio State University Department of Anthropology in 1987 produced several artifacts from the mound's vicinity, but the evidence does not change or alter current perceptions of the mound with regard to age or function.

One reason we know so little about the Alligator or any of the mounds and earthworks in this area is that no one has ever bothered to investigate the sites thoroughly. We have spent over a hundred years speculating, often wildly, rather than meticulously investigating the places where people lived and worked.

The thorough scientific investigation of the area could lead to a more complete understanding of not only the Alligator Mound but of all the mounds in the region. To date, the most comprehensively investigated Hopewell (Middle Woodland) habitation site in Ohio is the Murphy Site (see Chapter IV). Continued work there and at other sites in the Granville area, will provide valuable information concerning the day-to-day lifestyles of the Moundbuilders of the Licking region. The insights offered by archaeological research at these habitation sites may in turn enhance our understanding and appreciation of ceremonial sites such as the Alligator Mound.

Suburban and urban development have radically altered the topography and environment surrounding the Alligator Mound since I first visited the site. This transformation has been documented in several thousand photographs taken of the Alligator Mound and the surrounding property (Figure 24) since 1983. A joint effort between photographer Kent Bowser of Santa Fe, New Mexico, and LCALS, the documentation project was undertaken to record the change from a predominantly rural landscape to one that is primarily urban. The visual record provided by the photographs will offer future generations a chance to study and respond to now-lost aspects of the Alligator Mound's relationship to the surrounding landscape, the physical context in which it was built and used.

Today the Alligator Mound has been incorporated into the landscape design of Bryn Du Woods Development, a housing subdivision built during the late 1980s and early 1990s. The developer has set the mound aside and preserved it in a one and one-half acre green space. No laws, state or federal, protected the mound, and the developer was under no obligation to save it. Yet had the community been more knowledgeable and sensitive to prehistoric sites such as the Alligator Mound, steps might have been taken to preserve and protect it fifty or a hundred years ago, perhaps on twenty or thirty acres as was done at Serpent Mound.

So many of the major sites in Licking County are gone: the Old Granville fort, the large circular enclosure by Clouse Lane, the crescent just southeast of the Alligator, the mound on Mount Parnassus, the mound that once stood at the intersection of Main Street and Broadway in Granville, not to mention the vast majority of mounds that once made up the Newark Earthworks. All of these mounds have disappeared with little or no written or visual documentation. Nonetheless, it is heartening that some significant sites remain. If the citizens of Licking County act soon and insist that these sites be included in the planning process, we may yet succeed in saving them.

Bowser

Figure 24   1985 Aerial View of the Alligator Mound

CHAPTER IX
PRESERVING THE PAST FOR THE FUTURE

Paul E. Hooge

At the present time, ninety percent of the known archaeological sites on federal land in the Four Corners area of the American Southwest have been looted. Almost all of the Mimbres sites in southern New Mexico have been vandalized. Thousands of sites in Arkansas and Louisiana have been destroyed through land leveling and looting over the past three decades, and in some areas of Arkansas few undisturbed sites remain.

One of the most-recent and best-publicized examples of the wholesale looting of an important archaeological site occurred in 1987 at Slack Farm in northwestern Kentucky. The site was a major Native American settlement from what is often called the "contact period" (A.D.1500–1650), the time of the first sustained contacts between American Indian and European populations. The individuals responsible for the destruction were artifact collectors and dealers from Kentucky, Indiana, and Illinois. Each had paid one thousand dollars to obtain the right to dig at Slack Farm. After the looting, Brian Fagan described the site as looking like a battlefield: "a morass of crude shovel holes and gaping trenches. Broken human bones litter the ground and fractured artifacts crunch under foot."

In most states, including Ohio, no laws prohibit the looting of archaeological sites unless they are located on federal or state land. This leaves most important archaeological sites in Ohio unprotected.

In Coshocton County, Ohio, an organized group of collectors allegedly carried out an undetected looting operation on public land over a five-year period in the late 1970s and early 1980s. Mohawk Dam Site No. 2, the site plundered by this operation, was probably occupied about 11,000 to 8,000 years ago during the Paleoindian and Early Archaic periods. The crater-filled area is now reminiscent of the scene Brian Fagan described at Slack Farm.

Knudson has expressed the view of many concerned avocational and professional archaeologists:

> What will archaeology in North America look like in 2050? Except for a few interesting curiosities and some library texts, archival records and museum collections, it may not exist by the middle of the twenty-first century. Unless there are some fundamental changes in North American Archaeology, 98% of all (not currently known) archaeological deposits will have been destroyed.

Knudson goes on to say that existing laws are so weak that they do not demonstrate a serious commitment to protecting archaeological sites as a part of the public trust. About two-thirds of the United States is open to unregulated collecting and destruction, and only five to seven percent of this area has been archaeologically surveyed. The first question we must address then is why Americans have not placed a high priority on protecting the nation's prehistoric heritage.

This chapter provides some background information on the problems that face archaeology today. Many of these problems are rooted in American ideas about property ownership and history, which are in turn based on such concepts as manifest destiny and on interpretations of Biblical text.

As we enter the quincentennial of Columbus' contact with the "New World," scholars from all over the world are conducting research that will eventually result in dramatic revisions of the history of the Americas. These revisions are meant to enlighten, not to condemn: to develop a more truthful and accurate understanding of our past. It is hoped that the ideas discussed in this chapter will stimulate thought about our perceptions of the past, about archaeology, and about the future of the archaeological resource in North America.

Property Ownership and the Roots of the Archaeological Crisis

Strictly speaking, therefore, there has never been in this country a dependent peasantry. The yeomanry are absolute owners of the soil which they tread; and by a more jealous watchfulness of their rights, and by a more steady spirit of resistance against every encroachment, than be found among any other people.

The passage above, quoted from C.M. Haar from an 1833 publication titled *Commentaries on the Constitution of the United States,* demonstrates the principles of land ownership that have long guided the legal system of the United States. The right of property owners to plan and execute in the best interest of their own future was incorporated into the Constitution and the Bill of Rights and considered almost sacred from the beginnings of nationhood. This attitude continues to be prevalent among many contemporary Americans.

In part, such principles developed out of a desire to avoid what the "founding fathers" saw as pitfalls in the English legal system. Under eighteenth-century English law, the Crown reserved the ownership of all heritage resources, including those on private land. In the United States, by contrast, the authors of the Constitution and Bill of Rights emphasized the rights of private landowners. They clearly defined the rights associated with private ownership in the "Taking Clause" of the Fifth Amendment, which states "nor shall private property be taken for public use without just compensation." The Fourteenth Amendment applies this legal concept to all states.

For the most part, the authors of the Constitution and the Bill of Rights were neither aware of nor concerned about the many archaeologically significant sites located throughout the land that eventually would be incorporated into the United States. Euro-American settlers had only begun to happen upon and so "discover" the mounds and earthworks of the Midwest and Southeast. Numerous other archaeological sites, including all those located west of the Mississippi, were unknown to the former colonists of the eastern seaboard. Not surprisingly, the ownership of such archaeological sites and the artifacts they might contain was not specifically addressed in these documents. Consequently, the archaeological heritage came to be regarded as part of the land and so subject to the rights of the private landowner. As American laws have evolved and been interpreted, everything in or on land—whether minerals and other natural resources or artifacts and other evidence that constitute the archaeological heritage—is considered to belong to the land's owner and so can be taken for public use, or protection, only under the previsions of the Fifth Amendment's Taking Clause. Thus, United States law fails to define ownership of archaeological resources as distinct from ownership of land.

Although laws have been implemented to protect archaeological sites on federal and state land, only a few states have laws that protect archaeological resources on private land. As Knudson points out, no legislation or policy statement protects archaeological sites of any type as part of the constitutional guarantees for the people's general welfare. The National Environmental Policy Act of 1979 does affirm that it is in the interest of the nation to preserve important historic, cultural, and natural sites, but archaeological resources are not clearly defined beyond this. Even archaeologists have been slow to advocate concepts of public responsibility and ownership for the archaeological heritage. Knudson states: "the archaeologists themselves have not understood the need to clarify the public nature of the resource base."

Many countries have worked to protect their historic and prehistoric heritages for longer than the United States. However, most efforts to insure long-term preservation have developed within the past two hundred years. A brief survey of a few such efforts reveals how those in other countries have sought to balance the public's collective right to the past with the rights of individual property owners.

In the mid-nineteenth century, Czechoslovakian historian Frantisek Palacky devised innovative plans for the study and preservation of that country's prehistoric and historic sites, fortifications, burial grounds, castles, and buildings. He demanded that careful records be kept because monuments cannot be recreated once they are destroyed. Palacky also sought to organize the collections at the national museum. At the time his plans were almost unique in their scope and in the thoroughness with which they provided a foundation for a national policy of preservation.

Even earlier, in 1807, the Crown Prince of Denmark had signed a series of recommendations intended to protect that country's prehistoric and historic heritage. His recommendations suggested that prehistoric sites be divided into two categories: those that because of their importance would have state protection and those that would to be left to the land owner's discretion. He also proposed that a state museum be built to house the nations archaeological objects for the benefit of the general populace. But the Prince did not stop with just these farsighted recommendations. He recognized the need for broad-based public understanding and appreciation of archaeological resources. In what may be the first official message supporting the idea of popular education in archaeology, he stated: "Some appropriate way must be found of informing the peasantry of the value of archaeological finds."

By the early twentieth century archaeology was part of the school curriculum in Denmark. At about the same time, references to archaeology began to appear with some frequency in popular literature, and archaeological publications became popular and widely available. Radio programming and then, after 1950, television also have been used to transmit messages and information about archaeology. Today, one out of every one hundred Danes subscribes to the popular archeological periodical, *Skalk*, and archaeologists are esteemed as respected professionals. Perhaps as a result of the high level of public awareness, Denmark protects archeological resources with great vigilance. Strict laws that are almost impossible to challenge or circumvent govern the protection and preservation of archaeological sites. Such laws are generally respected by Danish citizens, and incidents of illegal looting and vandalism are virtually unknown. Denmark's tradition of public support for archaeology and community respect for archaeological resources is perhaps the strongest anywhere.

Given the British legal traditions regarding ownership of heritage resources, one might have expected Great Britain to be a leader in establishing policies for national archaeological preservation, but such is not the case. Historical and archaeological research has long interested many amateur and professional British scholars, as is evident in the enormous and varied collections of national institutions such as the

British Museum. In fact, by contemporary standards, British scholars and adventurers might be said to have "looted" much of the world in their zealous acquisition of "treasures" such as the Elgin Marbles of the Parthenon. But this interest did not translate into early or widespread legal protection for archaeological sites in Britain. Nor did it lead to the kind of public support for archaeology found, for example, in Denmark.

One of the major problems in Great Britain has been a complacent or even negative public attitude toward archaeology. This attitude exists because education has been grossly neglected by professional archaeologists and conservationists. Only in the last few years have major steps been taken to correct these problems

These few examples reveal that preservation of archaeological sites in other western nations does not follow any consistent or predictable pattern. Nonetheless, a few tentative conclusions can be suggested. The concept of public ownership of archaeological resources seems to occur most frequently in countries where the current inhabitants are the descendants of those who occupied the area over a long period, perhaps over several millennia. Smaller and more ethnically homogenous populations, such as that of Denmark, might be more prone to preserve cultural sites, especially ancient ones, because contemporary citizens perceive the individuals who created and occupied the sites as direct ancestors and so feel a stronger sense of proprietorship toward the sites. It also seems clear that education can play a major role in developing public appreciation for the archaeological heritage. Where traditions of private landowners' rights are strongly developed, public awareness is particularly significant in nuturing an equally strong sense of public ownership and responsibility for archaeological resources.

If one is willing to accept these propositions, it becomes apparent that preservation efforts in the United States face many challenges. Legal traditions emphasizing the rights of individual property owners and the existence of an incredibly non-heterogenous population scattered over an immense land mass make it difficult to foster the concepts of public ownership and cultural continuity that might lead to greater public appreciation of archaeological resources. Such difficulties must be addressed and surmounted before we can achieve success in enforcing existing preservation legislation or in enacting more comprehensive preservation policies.

Attitudes Toward Land Use

Many contemporary thinkers in a wide range of fields have become concerned about long-prevailing attitudes toward the natural and cultural resources of the earth—attitudes that have valued short-term over long-term considerations and individual rights over shared responsibilities. To some observers, such attitudes have precipitated a global crisis in the way land and resources are used: often with little respect for the fragile balances that allow life to exist. In a widely read article published in *Science* in 1967, philosopher Lyn White asserted that the roots of the worldwide land-use crisis could be attributed to the rise of Judeo-Christian religious philosophy. According to White, Judeo-Christian beliefs that humans have dominion over nature and a God-given right to make the land over as they please have led to the concept that property owners have the unchallenged right to use such property as they see fit.

Few of the individuals who have commented on White's treatise agree with it completely. One issue is that the texts White cites can be translated and interpreted in a variety of ways. Some commentators have suggested that the problems White attributes to Judeo-Christian religious beliefs might have developed instead from misinterpretations which removed phrases such as "dominion over" and "man in the image of God" from their proper spiritual context. Nevertheless, White's theories offer a interesting perspective on the ideas that have determined and guided traditions of land use and property ownership in the United States.

The concepts of property rights reflected in the American Constitution and Bill of Rights synthesized the previously mentioned desire to correct what were seen as problems or inequities in English law with more basic precepts derived from the authors' shared philosophical and religious beliefs, which were in turn often based on the Judeo-Christian attitudes described by White. Later interpretations of property rights draw on these same sources. Certainly the belief that humans have complete dominion over the land seems to have been incorporated into American ideas regarding land use and ownership from the time of the nation's founding. And this belief was often expressed in religious terms, as if it were part of a divine order or plan.

Many American sermons and religious writings, especially from the eighteenth and nineteen century, might be cited to support this interpretation, as Denison University professor Tony Stoneburner has proposed. The religious underpinnings of the philosophy of domination over the land are apparent, for example, in a 1787 sermon delivered at Marietta, Ohio, by Manasseh Cutler:

> To behold a country which was lately, very lately, a howling wilderness, the gloomy abode of numerous savage tribes, the haunts and lurking places of the cruel invaders of our defenseless frontiers... a people ignorant of the true God and devoted to their heathen rights and barbarious superstitions; to see this country so rapidly changing into cultivated fields, inhabited by civil and well-regulated societies, peaceably enjoying the fruits of their enterprise, industry, culture and commerce... (cited in Cutler & Cutler, 1888, p. 13).

Cutler's words imply that the transformation of "howling wilderness" into "cultivated fields" was a mission supported, almost demanded, by God. Similarly, the natural bounty of the North American continent was often seen as a special blessing, a new Jerusalem, given by God to a chosen people: the Euro-American settlers. As settlers moved into and eventually across the country, these religious or quasi-religious beliefs could be used to justify, even if unconsciously, almost any action taken to "tame" the land and "civilize" its former occupants. The incredible labor involved in carving civilization out of wilderness also gave rise to another perception: that through their labor the pioneers obtained certain rights of conquest over the land and that those rights could be passed on from one generation to the other.

Taken together with faith in the seemingly inexhaustible supply of land on the continent, the beliefs and philosophies described here led many Americans to accord privileged and almost sacred status to the rights of property owners to use, exploit, and even destroy their land and the resources it might contain. No matter how sincerely held and how understandable these beliefs may have been in the historical framework in which they developed, perhaps it is now time, as White and others have suggested, to consider their consequences. Despite their long traditions, the ideas that have conventionally governed land use may no longer be viable as we approach the twenty-first century.

Euro-American Perceptions of Native Americans

Over the past few centuries, Americans have had conflicting, if equally stereotyped, views of Native Americans. On the one hand seen as the "noble savage" and keeper of the forest, the Indians were more frequently portrayed as primitive peoples unsuitable as stewards and managers of the vast and richly endowed American landmass. When asked whether Native Americans were perceived by Euro-Americans to be part of their past, Dr. James B. Griffin, a senior research associate at the Smithsonian Institute, replied:

> Only when they neglected to give up their land easily. They had a strange idea that this country belonged to them, you see. It seems absurd but they did have that feeling about their homes. The European treatment of the Indians has been a great tribute to the real values of Christianity [which are] grab it, if you can take it, take it. It was God's will that these heathens should have to give up their land. (LCALS, 1986b)

Despite the massive pandemic of European diseases that in some cases all but wiped out entire populations, the Native Americans continued to fight white expansion and military force tenaciously and refused to have their lives dominated by the invaders. The peaceful settlement of a "virgin" and "empty" land was hardly peaceful.

Most of the historical record—compiled in large part by Euro-Americans— identifies the Native American as a hunter: bold, wild, independent, but also savage, hostile, and frequently cruel. Native Americans are seldom shown as farmers tending crops, as peoples with complex social and political structures, or as creative in the arts and capable of implementing abrupt changes in concepts and lifestyle—although they were, and are, all these things. Many writers now agree that it was not in the interest of the United States to portray Native Americans as civilized, cultured, or capable of properly managing the lands on which they lived. It was far easier to see them as nomadic, unsettled hunters whose demise and subjugation were only part of the natural process of the advance of "civilization," understood as Western Civilization.

The misconceptions that have resulted from such stereotypes have severely hampered understanding of the prehistory and history of the Americas. Only in the mid-twentieth century, for example, did archaeologists began to realize that all the major advances in agriculture, pottery, metal working, and textiles were not imported from Mesoamerica or Siberia. Perceptions of North American Indians as "uncreative and stupid" had blinded scholars to evidence of innovations having developed in this part of the hemisphere. The "discovery" of the mounds and earthworks posed other problems for American settlers and scholars of earlier generations. Many refused to connect these examples of sophisticated engineering and building with the ancestors of the Native North Americans, perhaps because doing so would have challenged their perceptions of local Native Americans as savages standing in the way of progress. One contemporary scholar summed up the situation as follows:

> Few Euro-Americans were prepared to interpret these finds as evidence of the creative abilities of North American Indians. The mounds and earthworks were accommodated with a primitive view of these Indians by claiming that they had been built by some vanished people, variously identified as Scandinavians, Hebrews, Toltecs, or Israelites. Such speculations easily became part of white American folklore in the nineteenth century since they accorded with the popular image of native people as blood-thirsty savages. (Trigger, 1986, p. 190).

Lingering stereotypes of Native Americans are still evident in literature,

films, television programs, and in the plethora of souvenirs found in the
trading posts (frequently white-owned) clustered along the tourist routes
of the American Southwest. There one can still see the image of the "noble
savage"—crafted in plastic on a plastic palomino—along with an array of
other material meant to bring forth some image of a colorful, peaceful,
primitive, and culturally static race. Today such stereotypes survive
almost as a defense mechanism: if the stereotypes are believed to be real
then perhaps the destruction of Native American peoples and cultures can
be accepted and justified as simply a natural process, ordained by either
God or destiny. Yet the wounds left by such destruction are still deep and,
in some places, open. In Wisconsin, Minnesota, Alaska, and other parts
of North America serious conflicts still exist between whites and Native
Americans over such issues as fishing and hunting privileges extended in
treaties as much as a century ago.

Methods for Preserving the Past

Several states and communities have seen fit to provide for their
prehistoric cultural heritage with legislated requirements for archaeological surveys and, in some cases, archaeological studies included in the
process of planning for development on private land. New Mexico has a
model archaeological ordinance for local governments that protects sites
on both public and private lands. Ann Arbor, Michigan, requires
archaeological surveying and planning, with a property's developer
paying for both the survey and, if necessary, compliance with regulations. Other communities have similar programs. In Dade County,
Florida, any structure built in violation of ordinances governing archaeological sites must be removed, and fines of up to five hundred dollars per
day can be levied against offenders. Larkspur, California, has a similar
ordinance. Despite these examples, however, only an extremely small
percentage of municipalities have archaeological ordinances. Through
new legislation (1991), the state of Arkansas now extends protection for
archaeological resources to both public and private lands. If enforced
properly, the law could almost eliminate the looting and desecration of

archaeological sites in that state.

Most scholars believe that the lack of protection for prehistoric sites derives at least in part from a general reluctance to challenge property owners' "inviolable" rights. Limitations placed on such rights by the conscious and purposeful regulation of development are relatively new phenomena, especially in democratic societies. In many ways, planning for the future environment is still in an experimental stage, and the techniques used to implement plans are still crude.

The problem with planning in general, according to Olaf Prufer, Professor of Anthropology at Kent State University, is inherent in our political system. Almost all planning at the city, county, state and federal level is done on the time frame of terms of political office. Most offices (mayor, governor, president, and others) are elected for limited terms, often of four years or less. Consequently, most planning is based upon that term of office. When office holders change after each election, new plans are formulated, frequently with little regard for what has gone before. As a result, there is little long-term continuity in planning. C.J. Berger sums up the difficulties encountered in planning in this way:

> Despite its claim to be an intellectual discipline, planning [in America] has evoked almost as many theoretical self-expressions as there are persons who practice the craft. On the pragmatic side, planners are caught between the nation's ambivalence toward long-range government planning, which still smacks of despised socialism to many, and the reality that planning underlines major investment and allocation decisions in every realm of personal, corporate, and administrative life.

Of the many forces that threaten archaeological sites, Berger identifies four that stand out as particularly serious. First, real estate economics, especially close to urban environments, raises the price of land to the point where it becomes financially unfeasible to preserve sites, unless the land is in public hands. Second, what Berger calls the "pursuit of progress syndrome" sacrifices the goal of preservation to combined forces of real estate and governmental interests that perceive their actions to be part of the practical necessity for change. A third force involves favoring private gain over community benefit in preservation through constitutional and property law doctrines. And finally, there is the failure of city, state, and federal governments to devise landmark programs that grapple realistically with the overriding preference of the legal system for private property rights.

The reluctance of the village of Granville to provide specific guidelines for preservation of the Alligator Mound can be offered as an illustration of the combined action of the four forces described by Berger. Once the land had been purchased with the intent to develop it, and once the village had extended its incorporated limits to include the mound, the value of the land rose beyond what most preservation-minded organizations would be able to spend in order to preserve the mound—that is if any group (including the village itself) had been interested enough to do so .

Instead, the village government welcomed the new development, and the case of the Alligator Mound fits Berger's "pursuit of progress syndrome." The expansion of the village and increasing its tax base were seen as overriding priorities. Although it would have been simple for the village to stipulate through an ordinance or through zoning that this and other sites be considered for preservation, it appears that no one wanted to challenge the right of the owner to use the land as he saw fit. The situation was also compromised by the owner's promise to preserve the site. No one challenged the property owner's right to determine how a site as important as this could or should be preserved.

We regulate the placement and size of signs, the location and appearance of buildings, the appearance and upkeep of properties, the appearance of transportation corridors, the removal of topsoil; we prevent the accumulation of junk in varying degrees and determine where junk can be dumped, we define trash and prevent its accumulation. The aim of such regulation is to create an environment that is enjoyable, visually pleasing, and clean—in a sense, aesthetic. If we go to such great efforts to regulate the size and placement of signs, it seems absurd that we refuse to give at least as much attention to protecting important remains of the past, which also have aesthetic qualities.

The concept of aesthetics as an important element in the quality of life of Americans was directly addressed in the National Environmental Policy Act of 1979. With regard to archaeological and historic sites it states...

> [to] assure for all Americans safe, healthy and aesthetically and culturally pleasing surroundings... [to] preserve important historic, cultural and natural aspects of our national heritage an maintain wherever possible an environment which supports diversity and variety of individual choice.

The Alligator Mound certainly fits into the visually aesthetic classification, but it also fits into a more cognitive classification. The mound's relationship to the past and present, as a connection to its builders' thought processes—their concepts of time, space, and universe—is worth preserving in the intellectual form of the mound as well as its physical form. It is true that at this time, we may not be able to define the builders' concepts of time, space and universe, but preserving the potential to know is surely a worthy thing to do.

Protecting Archaeological Sites at the State Level

Archaeological sites on state properties are handled independently by each state, but any state project with federal funding must comply with federal laws regarding archaeological resources in the same way that private projects do.

Washington State has some of the toughest state laws, in many ways as strict as those at the federal level. The most common state regulation for both state property and private property today is related to human remains. Currently, thirty-one states regulate the excavation or possession of human remains to some degree. The manner in which Native American remains are treated is one of the most volatile issues in archaeology today. Several states have enacted new legislation regarding human burials: Arkansas, Connecticut, Delaware, Michigan, New Mexico, Oklahoma, Ohio, Washington and others have made additions to strengthen existing legislation regarding human remains. Federal legislation has recently been passed that provides protection for Native American burial sites in every state; the law also includes protection of artifacts associated with a burial.

Although the reburial issue has not generally had a serious impact on preservation of sites on private property it is important to consider that the human remains and prehistoric material culture issues are so strong today they may influence what happens to sites on privately owned land in the future, especially in states with large Native American populations.

All fifty states regulate archaeological sites on their property and require that any excavations be done by qualified archaeologists with a state-issued permit. No states permit the collection of prehistoric artifacts on state lands. Several states (Arkansas, Illinois, Louisiana, Washington) require that artifacts excavated on state lands become the property of the state or must remain in a qualified institution.

Ohio's archaeological resources are protected only if they are on state or federal lands. But there are a variety of methods available for preserving sites in private property through enabling legislation. Since 1913, Ohio has reserved the right to acquire archaeological properties through eminent domain (section 1743.07 Ohio Revised Code). Essentially, this law was intended to allow incorporated preservation-oriented organizations to acquire sites through "a taking" if it was the only method for acquiring the site. The law today implies that only the Ohio Historical Society may use this legislation. This potentially powerful preservation tool has never been used, which is a testimonial to the even more powerful resistance to the use of eminent domain to take private property.

Section 1743.07 was enacted out of concern for the future of many important archaeological properties in Ohio. Many highly respected nineteenth-century antiquarians and archaeologists like Professor F. Wright, Ephraim Squire and Edwin Davis, Isaac Smucker, and Frederick W. Putnam had all voiced concerns about the future of such sites as the Alligator Mound, the Newark Earthworks, Mound City, and dozens of other sites. The effort to establish legislation that would guarantee preservation failed because no one was willing to use the law.

If the preservation of archaeological sites on private land in Ohio is to take place it will have to be done through enabling legislation contained in the Ohio Revised Code, through other voluntary means or through the purchase of the sites (which implies a willing land owner).

The state, through the Revised Code, does provide mechanisms for creating a greater awareness of the significance of archaeological resources. The State Registry Program could help property owners understand the significance of the sites on their land and create a greater community awareness of the resource locally. The site marking system (Section 149.30) could serve some of the same functions as the registry.

The test of the usefulness of any legislation or program is whether or not it can be employed productively. The revised code says the state shall maintain a state registry of archaeological landmarks, establish a marking system to identify all designated archaeological sites in the state, try to acquire properties adjacent or contiguous to sites under control of the Society, acquire and hold conservation easements, and acquire and hold properties as archaeological preserves.

All of the above mechanisms and programs are useful and could lead to a greater number of temporarily and permanently preserved sites as well as a greater number of registered or listed sites. However, the state archaeological survey program is a passive or reactionary one and is not aggressively pursued.

The marking system is also passive and only used when the Society is approached by the landowner, who must purchase the sign. The Ohio Historical Society holds no archaeological easements and no archaeological preserves, although they are currently working on establishing a preserve in the New Albany area in cooperation with the Ohio Department of Natural Resources and the land owner. I could find no evidence of any other archaeological easements or preserves within the state, although sites have been preserved incidentally as parts of parks and recreation areas. For example the Franklin County Park System owns the earthworks at Highbanks Park. Significantly, little if any interpretation of the prehistoric features is attempted at Highbanks. The mounds and embankments are unmarked and could easily be missed entirely by the casual visitor. Other protected sites are found in the Cleveland/Akron and Lorain Metro Parks systems. Many municipalities that have extensive undeveloped properties will have some archaeological sites on these properties.

However, there is no state law that protects these sites. I was not able to locate evidence that any cities in Ohio have ordinances protecting archaeological sites although several cities in other parts of the country do as was noted earlier.

The city of Moraine, Ohio owns the Rausher-Bollander Earthwork (rectangular). About forty percent of the site and a burial mound within the enclosure were bulldozed to "make room" for a housing development. The Dayton Museum of Natural History holds the archaeological rights to the site.

One of the difficulties in assessing the preservation situation in Ohio is that no one has done a comprehensive study of the preservation situation. We need to know what laws or enacted legislation have been used, what sites have been preserved and through what methods, and what is the attitude of the public toward preservation.

There appears to be little effort to actively preserve sites on private property in Ohio, except by the Archaeological Conservancy of the United States. The Ohio Historic Society and the State Historical Preservation Office currently play passive roles in site preservation. The Preservation Office maintains a lower profile because of financial problems and the Historical Society has not established site preservation as a priority within the education department where archaeology is housed. The problem is not simply one of funding, but of priorities.

Conclusion

If we do not establish for the public the value of archaeological research, and the preservation and conservation of the resource, then we will lose the resource. Archaeologists must learn more about public attitudes regarding archaeology so programs can be developed that will correct misconceptions and instill a preservation/conservation ethic.

Archaeologists must work more closely with Native Americans, stress the importance of archaeology to other sciences (biology, anatomy, ecology, botany), educate the public about the scientific process, and provide the public with a perspective on cultural evolution.

One reason there is no archaeological conservation or preservation ethic generally within the public is because, in the past, archaeologists have seen little value in transmitting information about their findings to Native Peoples or the general public. Presently, there is more interest in sensational claims about Atlantis, Noah's Ark, Tutankhamen's curse or Nazca lines as landing strips for visitors from outer space than in serious archaeological pursuits.

There are several reasons why archaeology is in trouble and why a general ethic for saving the resource has not developed. First, is the "deeply held American opposition to anything that stands in the way of progress." Second, Americans have never accepted America's prehistoric past as their own, and third, artifacts are considered to be scientific specimens or aesthetic items whose meaning is lost in a search for formal qualities and monetary values. They are not seen as humanistic documents that can become pieces of a "text" if property excavated and evaluated by a professional.

Most of the writers who have addressed this issue agree that America's preoccupation with money has been an encumbrance to preservation and conservation in archaeology (and ecology). It seems as if Americans generally place little value on the intellectual and aesthetic unless it can earn interest. Preservation is most successful when it can generate income.

Preserving and conserving archaeological resources is a relatively new value or ethic for Americans. Preserving large numbers of prehistoric sites on private property is a concept that is only two decades old.

There is considerable resistance to legislated preservation or conservation for private archaeological sites. Americans generally feel that restrictions placed on their ability to determine how their property will be used is a violation of their constitutional rights, although they have been accepting these restrictions for several decades through zoning and other regulations. There is no general consensus within the archaeological community concerning how to protect sites on private property. Generally, it is thought that education is politically the safest way to encourage preservation through the establishment of a public ethic. However, education will take years to accomplish and thousands of sites will be lost along the way.

In Licking County alone there are tens of thousands of prehistoric sites, marking the camps, villages, quarries and burial grounds of Native Americans who occupied the area for at least twelve thousand years. The absence of protective legislation means that hundreds of important sites will be destroyed with few or none being preserved or studied.

It seems ironic that we have arrived at a time when our technology will help us solve many of the great mysteries of America's archaeological past, but also a time when we are on the verge of destroying the resource before we can employ the technology to benefit ourselves as well as the resources.

Solving the problems described in this chapter will depend on how quickly Americans can be made aware of the archaeological dilemma. The challenge to the resource seems monumental; however, several national organizations have joined together to confront the problems and progress is being made toward finding solutions. In addition, there seems to be an increasing interest among the general population about the Native American's rich heritage of this country. Hopefully a greater awareness about the resource through education will provide the support needed to safely secure the most important sites for future generations and enable archaeologists to investigate many of those that will be destroyed through various land alteration processes.

GUIDE TO FURTHER READING

Berger, C. J. (1983), 3rd Ed. Land Ownership and Use, Boston, Ma. Little Brown and Company

Brenneman, R. L., Bates, S.M. (1984), Eds. Land Saving Action. Lovelo Ca. Island Press.

Brose, D.S., Brown, S.A., and Penney, D.W. (1986). Ancient Art of the American Woodland Indians. New York: Harry N. Abrams and Detroit Institute of Arts.

Brose, D. and Greber, N. (1979). Hopewell Archaeology: the Chillicothie Conference. Kent State University Press. Kent OH.

Bushnell, H. (1929). The History of Granville and Licking County. Columbus, OH. Hann and Adair.

Cleere, H. (1984). Great Britain. Approachable to the Archaeological Heritage: A comparitive Study of World Cultural Resource Management Systems, ed. H. Cleere. New York, NY: Caimbridge University Press.

Cowan, W. (1987). First Farmers of the Middle Ohio Valley. Cincinnati Museum of Natural History. Cincinnati, Ohio.

Cutler, W.P. and Cutler, J.P. (1888) Life Journals and correspondance of Rev. Mannssch Cutler. L.C.D. (Vol II). Cincinnati, OH. Robert Clark.

Dancey, W.S. (1991). A Middle Woodland Settlement in Central Ohio: A Preliminary Report on the Murphy Site (33 LI212). Pennsylvania Archaeologist, Vol. 61, No.2.

Fagan, B. (1988). Black Day at Slack Farm, Archeology, 41:4. PP. 15-16.

Farnsworth, U. and Emerson, T. (1986). <u>Early Woodland Archaeology</u>, Kampsville, Ill., Center for American Archaeology Press.

Fowke, G. (1902). <u>Archaeological History of Ohio</u>. Ohio State Archaeological and Historical Society, Columbus, OH.

Green, E. L. (1984), Ed. <u>Ethics and Values in Archaeology.</u> New York, N.Y. The Free Press.

Gyrisco, G. M. (1980). <u>Legal Tools to Preserve Archaeological Sites.</u> Informational pamphlet no. 11593, US Department of the Interior, National Park Service. Washignton, D.C.

Harr, C.M. (1976). <u>Land use Planning: A Casebook on the use, Misuse and Reuse of Urban Land</u>, Third edition. Boston MA: Little Brown and Co.

Herscher, E. (1989). A Future in Ruins. <u>Archaeology</u>, January/February 42:1 PP. 67–70.

Hively, R. and Horn, R. (1982). Geometry and Astronomy in Prehistoric Ohio. <u>Journal for the History of Astronomy.</u> Supplement, Archaeoastronomy 4; S1–S4

Holden, R. (1984). Moon Maze; Native American Earthworks Sculpt Lunar Oddyssey. <u>Earchamitte</u> 105 (1): 8–12.

Hooge, P. E. (1985) <u>Discovering the Prehistoric Mound Builders Of Licking County, Ohio.</u> Newark, OH: Licking County Archaeology and Landmarks Society.

Hooge, P. E. (1987). <u>Toward Education and Preservation: A Case Study of The Alligator Mound, Licking County, Ohio</u>. An Unpublished Masters Thesis. The Ohio State University, Columbus, Ohio. (Newark and Granville Public Libraries).

Hooge P.E. (Director). 1986(b). *Ethics and Archaeology (Part I).*
Conflicts in Collecting [videotape]. Licking County Archaeology and
Landmarks Society (Producer), Newark, OH:

Knudson, R. (1986). Contemporary Cultural Resource Management.
American Archaeology Past and Present. Eds. D. Meltzer, D Fowler,
J. Salboff. Washington D.C.: Smithsonian Press.

Knudson, R. (1989). North Americas Threatened Heritage. Archaeology, January/February, 42:1, P:71

Jennings, J. D. (1974). Prehistory of North America. Second Edition
McGraw–Hill, New York.

Lepper, B. T. An Historical Review of Archaeological Research at the
Newark Earthworks. Journal of the Steward Anthropological Society
18 (H2): 118–140.

Leonard, J. N. (1973). The First Farmers. Time Life Books. New
York, New York.

MacLean, J.P. (1879) The Mound Builders. Cincinnati: Robert
Clark.

McGinsey, C.R. (1972). Public Archaeology. New York: Seminar
Press.

Meltzer, D. J. , Fowler, D.D. and Tabloff, J.A. Eds. (1986) American
Archaeology Past and Future. Washington D.C. London Smithsonian
Institution Press.

Messenger, P. M. (1989), Ed. The Ethics of Collecting Cultural Property. Albuqerque, NM. University of New Mexico Press.

Rindos, D. (1984). The Origins of Agriculture. Academic Press. New York, New York.

Seeman, M. F. (1979). The Hopewell Interaction Sphere: The Evidence for Interregional Trade and Structural Complexity. Prehistory Research Series. 5(2) Indiana Historical Society, Indanapolis

Silverberg, R. (1986). The Mound Builders. Athens, OH: Ohio University Press.

Smucker, I. (1875). Scrapbook(Vol. I and II). Unpublished Collection Archived at The Granville Public Library. Granville, OH.

Squier, E. G. and Davis, E. H. (1848). Ancient Monuments of the Mississippi Valley. (Vol. I in the Smithsonian Contributions of Knowledge). New York: Bartlett and Weiford.

Trigger, B.G. (1989). Prehistoric Archaeology and American Society. American Archaeology Past and Present, eds. D. Metzer, D Fowler, J. Sabloff. Washington D.C: Smithsonian Press.

Wymer, D. A. (1988). Woodland Paleoethnobotany of the Ohio Valley Appalachaian Plateau. Paper presented at the Southeastern Archaeological Conference. New Orleans, Louisiana.

Wymer, D.A. (1987). The Paleoethnobotanical Record in Central Ohio 100B.C. to 800 AD: Subsistence Continuity Amid Cultural Change. Unpublished Dissertation, Ohio State University. Columbus, OH.

GLOSSARY

Archaeobotanical - Plant remains that are part of the archaeological record.

Archaeology - The scientific study of past life through the objects left by humans.

Amaranthus - Also called pigweed and careless — weed. A weed common to North America and used as a food resource by prehistoric and historic indians. Both the green leaves and seeds can be eaten.

Artifact - Any object made or modified by humans.

Assemblage - A collection of artifacts.

Atlatl - A device used to throw a spear.

Attribute - A well defined characteristic of an artifact that cannot be divided.

Austere - Very simple lifestyle, harsh, rigorous.

Bifacially flaked - Flaked or knapped on two sides - A spear is an example.

Bladelet - A thin narrow and uniform flake from a prepared chert (flint) core. Prized for their razor sharp edges.

Carbonized - Charred by fire.

Ceramics - Things made from fired clay (pottery).

Chronology - The science that deals with determining the dates and order of events.

Confluence - The point where two or more streams flow together.

Context - The relationship of artifacts and other cultural remains to each other and to the surrounding soil they are located in.

Cultivate - To grow, tend or plow.

Cultural item - An artifact, something made or altered by humans.

Culture - A learned behavior; all the beliefs, characteristics and customs of a group of people.

Deciduous - A broad leaf bearing plant or tree, oak, maple etc.

Diagnostic - A distinctive mark or characteristic which permits assigning an artifact to a particular time or culture.

Dispersed - Spread out over a given area.

Domestic settlement - A habitation or area where humans establish their homes or living area.

Glaciation - The accumulation and movement of ice over the surface of the earth.

Goosefoot - Also called pigweed, or lambs - quarter. A mild tasting green plant. The leaves were eaten as were the seeds. Domesticated and used as a crop food by prehistoric Native Americans.

Grid - A set of squares (checkerboard) used as a tool to establish the precise location of artifacts and features within an archaeological site.

Habitation - Environment in which an organism exists.

Habitation site - A site where people have lived.

Hunting and Gathering - A method of obtaining food through hunting and collecting edible plants.

Mica - A thin rattle - like, mineral that separates easily into thin translucent or transparent layers.

Middle Woodland - A period of time from 100 B.C. to 400 A.D. In some areas of North America it is referred to as Hopewell, but it is not limited by that single cultural affiliation.

Mortuary practices - The rituals and ceremonies associated with burying the dead.

Plow zone - The portion of a cultivated field that has been disturbed by a plow.

Post mold - The imprint left by a post in the soil.

Projectile point - Any shaped piece of stone, bone or antler, wood, etc. Used as the tip of a spear ar arrow.

Tropical cultigens - Plants domesticated in tropical environments, especially from Central and South America.

Viburnum - A member of the honey suckle family. Used in prehistory for food and perhaps medical purposes.